How to Help Your
Learning-Challenged Child
Be a Winner

How to Help Your
Learning-Challenged Child
Be a Winner

Dr. Robert E. Duke

New Horizon Press
Far Hills, New Jersey

Library of Congress Catalog Card Number: 92-63125

Duke, Robert E.
    How to Help Your Learning-Challenged Child Be a Winner

ISBN: 0-88282-076-1
New Horizon Press

Manufactured in the U.S.A.

1997 1996 1995 1994 1993 / 5 4 3 2 1

Contents

Why Children Fail

Born free of anxieties and with great capacities for learning and creating, children, especially those with learning disabilities, learn from adults to expect failure. Their capabilities are often blunted by parents and teachers who fail to realize that every child, whether learning-disabled or not, has a great capacity to grow, learn, and create.

Failure begins for many children with learning problems when they are as young as three years old and interacting with the adults who care for them. Children sense anxieties in adults and frequently adopt these anxieties as if they were their own. As children grow older, they begin to worry about meeting adult expectations. For children with learning disabilities these worries become *frustrations,* as they perceive failure in their efforts to please adults.

When children are chronologically old enough, they are admitted to school. Admission is determined by age. Maturity hardly ever enters into the determination. Schools are regimented, and children, regardless of their differences, are expected to fit into the slots *awaiting them.* Children are generally expected to be ready to read at the same age. Few schools pay attention to their maturational or other differences.

Schools are supposed to be magic places where children go to learn, to be happy, and to succeed—*not to learn how to fail.* A school should inculcate within each child a feeling of being successful. It should never be allowed to become a boring institution, to create a frustrated child, and especially not to create emotionally disturbed children or children who feel themselves failures. Yet many children learn these feelings in school.

This book offers suggested solutions to many of the educational and psychological problems that confront learning-challenged children and their parents. It is divided into several parts, each of which is concerned with solving these children's problems in specific areas. It indicts school systems whose current practices harm such children by causing many of them to fail, as happens with inept curriculums and poor disciplinary procedures. This book explains *why* those with learning disabilities fail in school and what can be done to help them.

This book also contains proposed solutions that can help resolve many of the psychological and educational problems which children with learning disabilities face as they grow up.

The mind of any person can be *improved* to a degree that far surpasses what is generally supposed. The importance of education and intellectual attainments is generally admitted, but few people know how to maximize that importance, especially in the case of children who are usually of average or above average intelligence but have learning disabilities. Too often, millions of dollars are spent every year and thousands of teachers are employed in vain.

This book will help you to:

- analyze the intellectual faculties of your learning-challenged child,
- improve your child's memory,
- educate your child despite learning disabilities,

- strengthen the intellect of your child,
- obtain knowledge.

There is nothing more important—no fact in nature of more intense delight and glory—than developing the mental capacities of these children.

One section of this book is devoted to innovations that, in my experience, have produced miracles for such children. The wonderful thing about these miracles is that you can repeat them with your own children. They are that simple to use. You may be able to do more for your child than any professional, simply because it is your own child with whom you will be working. This is not to say that children with learning disabilities don't need expert help. They do. But there will never be a substitute for the loving relationships that exist between concerned parents and their children. This love is important to the innovative procedures that you can use to solve your learning-challenged child's educational and psychological problems.

Many children with learning problems become tense and anxious, further intensifying their problems. I will explain techniques that you can use to help your learning-disabled child overcome anxieties and the accompanying body tensions. You will learn how to release your children from the emotional hang-ups that prevent them from making the progress of which they are capable. You will learn how to help them cope with the pressures of their world.

The prescription section contains proposed solutions for educational/psychological difficulties. You will rediscover some practical, time-honored everyday ideas, along with some new ones. They can help your learning-disabled children make the right adjustments to their problems while at the beginning of their lives, not after the problems have become so ingrained that they are difficult to solve. These are the years spent in the elementary school. They are the trusting years and should be the most productive educational years of a child's life. They are the foundation years, the years when the greatest effort must be put forth to guide a child. They are the receptive years when children are most amenable to adult suggestions.

During the elementary years, you—as parents—are most influential. Later, children are apt to be confused by the mandated body changes as they face puberty. For most children, the adolescent years are lonely years, because, within growing bodies, children yearn for lost childhoods. This is especially true for a learning-disabled child who, in adolescence, learns to feel a sense of failure more acutely.

The first part of the book is an admission that many of the growing child's problems can be blamed upon poor educational practices. Grading a young child is a common and harmful practice. Trying to teach a young child to read phonetically can be disastrous if the child is one with learning disabilities and lacks a special phonetic sense. You are encouraged to take a good look at *what teachers are doing to your child.*

The elementary school is the fountainhead of formal education; it should be a child's *golden years,* the most constructive part of a child's life. What happens to your child in the elementary school will determine whether the educational harvest will be fruitful or barren.

The elementary years are the habit forming years, when the child, especially the learning-challenged, should learn good study habits; when ambition should be gained and growth into a self-sustaining adult should begin.

A common thread binds this book together. It is a call for a total positive approach to your learning-challenged child. Children need this. Negative comments destroy children. Unfortunately, there are teachers who depreciate children with learning disabilities. If this happens to your child, you must neutralize the teacher's mistakes. You can do this with some of the solutions I propose.

An elementary school should be a positive factor in every child's life, whether or not that child has learning disabilities. If it isn't, there is something wrong with the school. Every school experience should be positive, because school children are in the process of acquiring the attitudes and values that will guide—or plague—them for the rest of their lives.

My work with children has been with those of both normal and retarded intelligence, many of whom had learning difficulties. The children in my school consistently averaged a year or better than children from other schools in the area, despite the fact that it was located in a disadvantaged section of town.

In addition to my other certificates, I am also a certified school psychologist in Massachusetts, where I worked with the psychiatric staff of the Boston Children's Hospital in the development of a projective personality test, Tasks of Emotional Development (TED). I also headed a private clinic for children with special problems.

The precious jewel of education cannot be purchased, nor obtained by proxy, nor inherited except in its rudiments, but must be cultivated by everyone for himself. This book is specifically designed to help you nurture, stimulate knowledge, and encourage the self-improvement of your children.

CHAPTER ONE

Learning

Children who have learning disabilities are not blind, deaf, or mute. They are not orthopedically handicapped. They are not health impaired, as is a person with a heart disorder. They are not mentally retarded, nor do they necessarily have behavior problems. Yet, at times, they can display any one or all of these symptoms.

The average language-challenged child is normally intelligent and possesses normal functioning sensory organs. Such children need to be in a classroom with their peers. Many have normal bodies, but sometimes do not behave like other normal children. How, then, can they be identified?

An individual with a learning disability has to learn to compensate for weak or troublesome areas, or else avoid them entirely. Some of us learned to use a typewriter in order to compensate for poor handwriting. I use a word processor together with a spelling check program because I still do not spell well. Most of us have minor learning problems and have learned how to handle them. Nelson Rockefeller, Woodrow Wilson, and Hans Christian Andersen are but a few who have overcome learning disabilities during their lifetimes. If your children are learning-disabled, don't let them give up. These individuals didn't.

Learning-disabled students lacking specific academic skills are unable to respond to the demands of their teachers and parents, producing a snowball effect. They may feel inadequate, insecure, anxious, and disorganized and be easily distracted. Many educators have realized that they can be distracted by "irrelevant and inappropriate stimuli," while some wonder if their "frequently reported distractibility and hyperactivity" can be laid to an aspect of their problem with selective attention.

If children's achievements do not correlate with their levels of intelligence, they may have specific learning disabilities which can be identified by testing either their oral expressions, their written expressions, their reading skills, or their math skills. If there is a *severe* discrepancy between a child's achievement and intelligence, a multi-disciplinary team should examine the child's physical condition for deficits in hearing, seeing, motor skills, and emotional disturbances.

Teachers can use any one of many test instruments to help them determine whether a student is dyslexic, among them the VMI, the BGT, the Detroit, the Wepman, the Slossen, and the Frostig. The trouble with these tests is that they are not reliable. They do not measure what they are supposed to measure, and they do not measure the same things in the same ways consistently. Many learning-disabled children exhibit common characteristics:

- short attention spans,
- excessive dependency upon parents or other adults,
- need for massive help and reassurance,
- negative or low self-concepts or feelings that they cannot achieve anything worthwhile,
- scholastic performances paralyzed by poor self-concepts.

In addition, there are several individual learning-disabled

characteristics. One obvious one is *perseveration,* characterized by continually repeating something when the repetition is no longer appropriate. These children call attention to themselves at a very early age. Teachers, when confronted with this type of disruptive child, should refer the child to the school psychologist. However, a quiet child, with similar learning-disabled problems, may be withdrawn and languish for lack of attention.

Children with learning disorders may also "act out" because of their frustration at not succeeding in school. When some bright children with learning disabilities find themselves grouped with children of low ability, they become bored. Some drop out of school, while others become overly aggressive and hyperactive. These symptoms also are obvious. But other children with learning problems become lethargic. They sit in their classrooms quietly, seemingly without being understood. Frequently, they are considered slow learners, but they aren't. They are children with specific problems that have been overlooked.

I recall one ten-year-old boy with multiple language deficits. His reading and other language skills were well below his grade level. His mother, who had tried to help solve his problems, probably assumed he was a dull child. She may have felt responsible for her son's educational deficits. The boy was referred to a well-known Boston clinic where he was labeled "dyslexic." I will never forget the relief this afforded his mother and teachers, for they had found something *outside the home and school* that could be blamed for his problems. I suspect that the boy himself felt some relief, too. He was no longer responsible for his reading problems; he had dyslexia. I saw less of his mother after that, perhaps because she felt less of a personal responsibility for her son's disability.

Dyslexia and other disabilities often cause *secondary* reasons for failure that become as difficult to overcome as the *primary* one. This secondary factor is always emotional, often causing teachers and parents to assume that a child is emotionally disturbed. In *Hypnotherapy for Troubled Children* (New Horizon Press, 1984), I described these secondary problems as a *vicious circle,* surrounding the original problem:

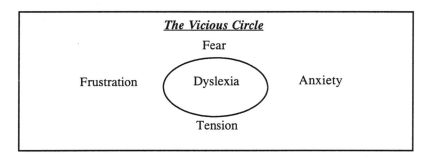

The Vicious Circle

Fear

Frustration   Dyslexia   Anxiety

Tension

In *Learning and Behavior Characteristics of Exceptional Children and Youth,* William I. Gardner refers to my *vicious circle* as "The Vicious Defeat Circle."

Peripheral, secondary factors are primary to helping a learning-challenged child. The mere presence of most exceptional learning and behavioral characteristics makes it more difficult for a child to be successful in achieving necessary reinforcement and positive emotional experiences. The more—or less—reinforcing events a child can obtain become unusually strong in influencing permanent behavioral characteristics. Problematic behavior patterns of any type are likely to produce negative reactions in the child's family and educational environments. The child is likely to develop self-concepts that interfere with his involvement in, and assimilation of, needed positive experiences. The child's inability to meet ordinary behavioral criteria further decreases the likelihood of a child's learning those social behaviors that will produce positive consequences.

Many times, learning disabilities not only produce emotional problems for children, but for their families as well. Indeed, the parents of a learning-disabled child sometimes have similar disabilities. When they do, the emotional problems surrounding their child also arouse emotional responses in parents, including a sense of gratitude for the help they themselves were denied being offered their child.

Characteristics of a Learning-Disabled Child

Many characteristics exhibited by those we call learning-disabled are traits that most children pass through as they mature. Many of us have occasionally reversed a letter in a word; some of us still do, but this does not constitute a learning disability.

Certain characteristics are significant whether they occur at an elementary, intermediate, junior or high school level:

- the parent has a similar problem,
- brothers or sisters have similar problems,
- the parent intuitively senses something is wrong.

The following characteristics are significant *only* at certain levels when they do not disappear with maturity:

I. Early Elementary

A. As a baby, the child has sleeping and feeding inconsistencies.
B. The child:
    1. clings to the mother and resists separation.
    2. was slow in learning to talk.
    3. can't seem to put puzzles together.
    4. has trouble walking, tiptoeing, standing on one leg, hopping on one foot, skipping, or walking a straight line.
    5. demonstrates poor balance on a balance beam.
    6. can't follow an object with its eyes.
    7. is decidedly awkward.

8. has problems copying geometric shapes.
9. cannot associate colors and shapes with their names.
10. acts like a baby at an inappropriate age.
11. consistently reverses letters.

II. Intermediate Grade Levels

A. The child:
1. lacks balance.
2. has trouble walking a straight line, tiptoeing, hopping, standing on one leg, or catching a ball.
3. can't follow an object with his eyes.
4. is decidedly awkward.
5. can't seem to see the paper to work on in spite of normal eyesight.
6. constantly rotates the paper.
7. writes with heavy pressure.
8. can't seem to distinguish left from right.
9. has trouble with shapes and colors.
10. reads one word at a time.
11. has trouble memorizing.
12. becomes nervous when asked to recite, despite knowing the answers.
13. starts working without waiting for appropriate instructions.

III. Junior and Senior High School

A. The student:
1. is failing academically.
2. is bored in school.
3. does not understand questions.
4. fails to see relationships.
5. fails to see how things are relevant.
6. withdraws socially.
7. joins peer misfits.

8. misbehaves in school.
9. is truant.
10. refuses needed aid.
11. displays poor judgment.
12. depends upon parents for simple things.
13. may appear bright, but receives failing grades.
14. doesn't turn in homework.
15. is moody.
16. stops trying.
17. plays with younger children.
18. is easily distracted.
19. does not include margins or headings on his papers.
20. bites nails, scratches body, plays with hair.
21. forgets directions.
22. has trouble moving from one task to another.
23. fails to finish assignments.
24. reverses letters and numbers.
25. has trouble forming sentences.
26. is inconsistent.
27. gets frustrated easily.
28. experiences sudden mood changes.
29. requires detailed explanations.
30. when reading, skips or mixes up words.
31. is overwhelmed by school work.

Dyslexia

Dyslexia is a word that teachers use to label the learning disability of some pupils. One aspect of dyslexia is reading problems. If children can remember what has been taught, if their oral vocabulary is well-established, if they can understand the theory behind phonetics but can't use it as they read, if they make progress then backslide to where they were before they made that progress—they are likely to be labeled dyslexic. Do they have trouble reading? Do they consistently reverse the letters in words and numbers? Do their words appear to be in the wrong order? If the answer to any of these questions is "yes," then the child may have dyslexia.

Dyslexia may be caused by genetics, or by a brain injury, and has many different levels of complexity. The less severe cases are not always noticed by teachers. The less affected child may simply fall behind peers and appear lazy and unintelligent. Eventually, such a child may become emotionally disturbed and/or drop out of school. Dyslexia is not completely understood, but psychologists, therapists, and remedial teachers can help an affected child. The younger children are when diagnosed, the more that can be done for them. Many dyslexic people are remarkably intelligent. Albert Einstein is a prime example of a brilliant dyslexic.

If you suspect that your child is dyslexic, the federal government will provide testing without charge. Different school systems offer various types of programs for dyslexic students ranging from special help in addition to regular classes to full-time placement in special classes. Different pupils require different programs. Each child's program should be tailored to specific needs. For more information, contact The Foundation for Children with Learning Disabilities, 99 Park Avenue, New York, New York 10016.

Word Phobia

I suggest another label for one of the problems that some children have with words: "word phobia." This label suggests the cause of the problem—some children are afraid of the words. The label *word phobia* suggests that the remedy for this reading problem is to be found with a psychologist, rather than with a reading specialist. In some cases, a psychologist is needed to uncover the dynamics that block the child's reading progress.

Many of the children with whom I have worked display symptoms of an emotional problem attached to the words they are to read. The harder these children try to read, the worse the emotional problem becomes. Finally, they accept the idea that they have dyslexia and can't read.

There are many different kinds of reading disabilities. Some children suffer developmental lags. Some children have perceptual disorders. Some children lack the sense modality required for reading. Some children can't identify sounds made right behind them, but can when the sounds are made in front of them. These children obviously have an auditory problem. Some children can't tell which one of their fingers you touch unless they see you doing it. Obviously, these children have a problem with tactual perception. Some children have physiological inadequacies, and their remediation must come from the medical profession. There is a large group of children existing in a gray area who hear well enough but can't understand what has been said; they have an auditory disability. These children usually have a difficult time expressing their thoughts. They may do well on oral quizzes but fail a written one, or they may fail in both dimensions.

There are different types of test instruments used in diagnosing children's problems. Some measure intelligence; others measure achievement, special interests, aptitudes, personality variations, and the like. Tests have been designed to screen children for just about everything, including learning disabilities. Teachers and psychologists use them to classify children for placement in appropriate groups for instruction. Some of these tests are diagnostic and help determine specific disabilities and suggest appropriate learning programs to help the student overcome those specific disabilities.

Ideally, medical doctors should be part of the educational teams that diagnose children's learning problems. They are the only people trained to determine if there is brain dysfunction from physical damage at birth, from an accident, or induced from a drug-abusing mother.

All phobic reactions are unrealistic responses to a stimulus of some kind. The phobic person has no conscious reason to be afraid; the reason resides in the subconscious mind. The phobia may exist because of a forgotten past experience. The subconscious part of the mind remembers, but it lacks the conscious part of the mind's ability to reason things out.

There are hundreds of types of phobias, ranging from agoraphobia (a fear of open spaces) to xenophobia (a fear of strangers) to zoophobia (a fear of animals). While fears are attached to specific situations, phobias are unrealistic and much more complicated. A child may develop a school phobia because a fearful mother unconsciously plants within the child her own fears of separation.

Phobias may come from a conscious attempt to cope with a real or imagined threat from within or without the individual. They are defense mechanisms. The phobic person holds on to his or her phobia because it is less threatening than the other danger. Usually, phobias result from one of three causes:

1. They may displace some more threatening anxiety.
2. They may defend the individual against a dangerous impulse.
3. They may result from conditioning.

Displacement dynamics cause most phobias. Stressful conditions that may create a phobia include school failure. Previous failure is a key factor in many learning disabilities. Children learn to expect failure by failing over and over again. They learn to hate school because it is *where* they fail. You can help these children by desensitizing them to failure, encouraging them, and avoiding criticism. Your child's fear of failing may be extinguished by a desensitizing through meditation therapy.

Fear of Failing

Anxious parents produce anxious children. Children normally want to please their parents and the other adults with whom they interact. In one way or another, they are always saying, "See me." What do you suppose happens to the child who is eager to please adults, but is only able to produce school work labeled "F" for failure? Do you think that saying "try harder" is going to do any good? The fact that the child has been told to try harder suggests an expected failure. The child may promise to "try harder," but a small voice inside seems to say, "You are going to fail." If the child expected to succeed, there would be no need to try harder. *The child would succeed because the child expected to do so.*

Word phobia effectively prevents a child from reading well. The school may decide that the services of a special teacher are needed, but, despite this extra effort, the child still may not do well. The extra effort only calls the child's attention to a reading problem: "They are doing this for me because I can't read." The successful teacher must find a way *around* the child's stumbling block (word phobia) if the child is to overcome it, learning to use the child's imagination in a positive way and desensitizing the child to the reading problem. Successful teachers must *misdirect* a child's attention around a learning block in order to overcome it. They must use their own imaginations, as well as those of the children they are trying to aid. A successful analogy would be a football coach who, upon finding his team facing a powerful defensive line too strong to crash through, sends the ball around the line or over the heads of his opponents.

Why is reading so hard for some children to learn? After all, they learned to talk before they got to school, and that is a much harder thing to do! Watching a learning-challenged child struggle in school, parents may well decide it was a good thing that they did learn to speak before entering the educational process—otherwise they might *never* have learned how.

A child who can't read is unhappy, and one may compensate by misbehaving, while another will simply *stop trying*.

Misdirection

Misdirection is a name I've given to a teaching technique that will overcome word phobia. You may have used it yourself. Haven't you misdirected children away from crying over some small abrasion by causing them to laugh at their favorite toy or pet?

During my undergraduate days, I entertained audiences with hypnosis tricks. Like many other entertainers, I used misdirection to shift the audience's attention away from what I was doing and on to something innocuous. I used placebos—sounds, flashing lights, and spinning discs—to distract the subjects and the audiences while I induced hypnosis. In a way, medical doctors do the same thing when they prescribe placebos for patients. Sometimes the placebos seem to do as well as any other medicines.

Misdirection and placebos are important parts of my hypnotic inductions. Some subjects are afraid of hypnosis. Some seem to have been conditioned to resist hypnosis. Misdirection works well with these reluctant subjects, and I have been able to induce hypnosis without their realizing it:

"You seem a little tense tonight. I have some pills [placebos] that will help you to relax. Please let me know when you begin to feel a little warm."

Hypnotherapists use many different types of inductions, but misdirection is the principal one, although many do not realize it.

The first rule of misdirection is to attach a power to some object to which the subject would most likely respond. As mentioned above, it can be a placebo, flashing lights, or the like. The reading teacher, or a parent, can misdirect the child's attention and get around a child's word phobia in the same way, and it doesn't take much ingenuity to do it.

Several years ago, I arranged a misdirection project with two groups of children who had learning problems. I informed the children that they were going to participate in a project to help them do better in math. They believed that the pills they were to receive would do wonderful things for them. I named the pills Obecalp (*placebo* spelled backward). The children were told to take one in the evening and one just before going to school in the morning. They were told this would improve their memories and concentration, that they could expect to relax and be less tense in school. I met with the children once a week for three or four months. They gathered in my living room, where we discussed their progress and practiced a little group hypnotherapy. The group taking Obecalp responded beautifully. One child, in particular, advanced far ahead of all the other children in his class. They all received benefits, but those who, in addition to having group therapy, took Obecalp made the most progress.

Helping a Learning-Challenged Child at Home

Begin by asking your child's teacher, "What skills are you teaching my child now? How can I help my child at home?" If necessary, insist upon answers.

You have a built-in knowledge of your child's habits, knowledge, and problems. Little children are usually interested in animals, magic, and other children, so begin with these things. Boys are traditionally more interested in stories about adventure, pirates, cowboys, explorers, and space. Girls are traditionally interested in stories about nature, animals, and myths, and, as they grow older, stories with a love interest. Girls mature about one and a half years before boys.

When your children are able to speak a few words, begin reading to them. Your child will enjoy the Mother Goose type of stories. Continue reading to your children as they mature. Your child should follow the printed words as you read them. You may be surprised to find that, before long, your child will be reading along with you. Something else worthwhile may happen: your child may become less addicted to television.

When your children begin to read independently, ask them questions about the stories they are reading. They will not only gain reading comprehensive abilities, but be open to guidance—especially if the stories they are reading have moral endings. Your library may sponsor a storytelling hour or have a children's section with a librarian trained to recommend books for your child. When your children can handle the responsibility, they should have their own library cards and accept the responsibilities that go along with them.

A fourth-grade child should have a good children's dictionary to look up words, and children in the fifth and sixth grades can make good use of children's encyclopedias. Encourage your child to develop the habit of looking things up by saying, "Let's look it up in the encyclopedia."

Your children will appreciate good children's books; however, don't be discouraged if they are also interested in comic books. Some of these are excellent and can lead your child into good reading habits. Some are exceptional, but many of them lack the cultural and ethical values that you may want your child to acquire. You must guide your child to those comic books that not only are enjoyable, but will also encourage emotionally healthy growth.

CHAPTER TWO

How We Learn

Most experts believe that a child's brain is essentially the same as an adult's and that it changes little during the growing-up years. The experts consider the brain to have two hemispheres; the front hemisphere produces language and the back hemisphere is responsible for understanding it. Many scientists believe that the trouble that sometimes exists between taking in language and understanding it exists because of a linking problem between these two hemispheres. This linking problem can be attributed to a lesion or injury that occurred at some time during the individual's development.

There is some evidence to indicate that we normally use both hemispheres, although a person with a language disability may have trouble extracting information from the right hemisphere, where language skills largely reside. But the evidence is not definitive.

Some experts believe that language deficits result from an abnormality in the sixteenth to the twentieth week in the development of the fetus. Another theory states that slow developing male hormones slow the development of the left hemisphere. This hypothesis is based upon the observation that language disabilities are more common in males than in females. My experience with children verifies this supposition. However, when male children reach the age of nine years, their hormone development correlates with their age to enable them to master the language skills that troubled them earlier, provided that they haven't picked up a *secondary psychological problem* that blocks language arts mastery.

Language disability may be familial, as there is a high incidence of similar deficits occurring in the same family. For some reason, lefthandedness is more apt to occur among the language-disabled. In 1979, the brain of a language-disabled person was examined and found to have a larger right hemisphere, but this singular sampling doesn't prove much. In the 1980s, researchers were trying to identify the part of the brain that controls functions. They found that contradictions exist. Today, some researchers believe that the right hemisphere is used for intuition and the left hemisphere for logic and that the two hemispheres do not interact with each other very well. They also believe that one hemisphere dominates the other.

Some scientists believe that the whole brain works like a hologram, a three-dimensional picture, with electrical or laser-like beams crossing over from left to right in order to form a perfect image. In this way, every cell is aware of what all the other cells are doing.

CAT scans reveal that mental activity occurs in different places for different individuals; not only that, there is mental activity occurring in places where it was not expected to occur.

Science still hasn't explained the way the brain functions. However, scientific research is bringing us closer to the right answers. We are confident that it won't be long before we will know how the brain receives, stores, processes, and transmits knowledge.

In the meantime, there are educational techniques that can help children overcome learning disabilities. In *Why Johnny Can't Read,* Rudolf Flesch blamed a lack of reading skills on a lack of phonetic skills. Many did not accept Flesch's premise. Around the same time, the term *dyslexia* was reinvented. Many teachers assumed that Johnny couldn't read because he suffered brain damage that resulted in his having perceptual problems. Today's reading teachers focus upon a number of *specified* learning disabilities.

School systems provide their teachers with reading books that are a part of a publisher's reading system. This reading system is called a *basal system*. A basal system offers a series of reading materials for each one of the elementary levels. Most systems use a phonic approach, whereby the children learn to sound out the words, along with a linguistic approach (whole-word or sight-word learning). These systems work well with the average pupil, but not with children who have learning disabilities. They require something different!

The Orton-Gillingham program and other programs were developed to fill this specific need. Such reading programs break down the process of learning to read into small steps that use every appropriate sense organ. Some researchers believe that dyslexia doesn't result from an inability to see the words but from an inability to remember their configuration.

Grace Fernald developed a system appropriately called the Fernald method. She joined the separate visual, tactile, auditory, and kinesthetic learning techniques into one comprehensive system. The Fernald method is still used; I used it extensively when I taught spelling to grade school children. My pupils traced their spelling words in the air and on paper. Together, we examined the configuration of the words and drew pictures about them. We used the words in sentences and wrote them collectively and individually. It didn't take long before the children could not only spell the words but, as a matter of course, read them.

The children looked at the words (visual), spoke the words (auditory), traced the words in the air and on paper (kinesthetic), and wrote the word (tactile). They used all their senses and effectively learned how to spell. Coincidentally, they also learned to read.

In the 1960s, the linguistic reading systems came into existence. These reading systems did not leave out phonetics, but delayed the sounding out of words until the children had acquired a large sight vocabulary. Children come to school with a large vocal vocabulary, and these books capitalized upon that fact. Most of the children's early reading vocabularies consisted of three-letter word combinations using a consonant, a short vowel, and another consonant. The children learned to read by becoming accustomed to their configurations. At first, the children became familiar with short and regular configurations; this was followed by irregular forms. These children learned to read short, easy stories. Most children were successful immediately. Meaning and word attack skills were taught *after* the children had successfully acquired a sight vocabulary of several hundred words.

Then a controversy developed. Some teachers wanted reading to begin with word attack skills (sounding them out). Other teachers wanted to have their children read for meaning from the beginning. The controversy continues.

Gattegno and Bannatyne found still another way to teach reading. They color-coded key letters to help pupils identify the different phonetic elements. This was an important addition to the teaching tools. The "A" sound as used in the word *spade* is represented by a blue-green color regardless of how it is spelled. It can be spelled *a, ei, ea,* and so on. The only trouble with the system is that some children are color blind; for them the system would have no advantage. But for the children who are not color blind, it remains an important teaching tool for children with learning problems.

Stern offers a novel way to teach reading. He writes on the blackboard sentences and stories that have been dictated by the children. The children hear the sounds of the words as their teacher says and writes them. This is a phonetic technique, and the children are able to see how their spoken words look. This technique can be used with the several other language-oriented subjects, such as spelling and writing. Stern's technique is recommended for language-disabled students.

Programmed teaching is popular. Usually, it is in workbooks or on video cassette. One advantage of programmed teaching is that the students can correct their own work immediately; usually, they cannot advance to the next level until they do. In this way, students progress step by step up through levels of increasing difficulty at their own pace, another appealing advantage for the language-disabled student.

Perceptual motor training began in earnest during the 1960s. Kephart was instrumental in this. He determined the levels of educational development for each of his pupils and began his remediation work at that determined and appropriate level. The child with visual/motor problems practiced random scribbling on the blackboard, did finger-painting, drew geometric figures, and so on to improve the use of the large muscle groups. Balance beams made their appearance in the classrooms, and the children walked on them to improve their sense of balance. This "movement education" resulted in children walking like ducks, making rabbit-like hops, and the like—all to help them develop balance. Kephart also worked to help children obtain better eye control. He moved objects back and forth before the children's eyes, and they followed these movements with their eyes.

Marianne Frostig developed a similar system. Frostig built her program around a series of special tests, each one designed to ferret out facets the child lacked and needed for his education. The child's education was modified toward his specific need. Later, additional tests determined if the child had improved in those defined areas. This program is controversial. Some educators claim that not all of the children identified as being perceptually handicapped had perceptual motor problems and, therefore, don't need that specialized training.

Doman and Delacato developed programs for brain injured children at their Institutes in Pennsylvania and New York. Delacato believes that the normal development of the human being is through a sequence of neurological steps, and, if one misses any of these steps, learning problems will result. These steps include rolling over, moving in a circle, backing up, crawling in several different directions, creeping, walking when holding on to something, walking without help, and walking in different ways. These are stages in the development of a child that most parents observe as their child matures. If a developmental problem exists, Doman and Delacato return the child to those elementary steps and then retrain him. Some brain-damaged individuals have been *patterned* to use the undamaged portion of their brains to establish new channels for the brain to stimulate muscle activity.

Today's remedial teachers seek to extinguish specific learning disabilities. Their remedial efforts are preceded by a testing program that defines the problem. For example, if a child has a visual-perceptual motor problem, exercises designed just for that problem are administered. The child might receive specific instruction in penmanship to coincide with the curriculum work taking place in the regular classroom. Specific remedial instruction is effective because it relates to specific classroom instruction. The classroom teacher is consulted daily by the special needs teacher to keep this relationship working. The child usually spends a small part of the day with the special needs teacher, but, during most of the day, remains in the regular classroom. This child keeps up with classmates and feels less isolated.

In *The Natural Way to Reading*, Nancy Stevenson suggests many fascinating yet simple methods to teach reading, many of which may be useful for learning-impaired children. Her system gives young readers keys with which to solve some of their reading problems. The keys consist of the following seven steps that help unravel problems associated with learning vowels, consonants, and the special words:

1. The teacher points to a word with a pencil and assists the child in counting the vowels: first vowel, second vowel, etc.
2. The child crosses out the second vowel to make it silent.
3. The child says the first vowel sound.
4. The child is asked to say the first letter sound and then to blend it (a consonant) with the long vowel sound, as *so* is in the word *soap*.
5. Should the child give a wrong answer, step 3 and 4 are repeated until he gets it right. If necessary, the teacher can prompt the child.
6. The child is asked to repeat the right sound.
7. The child is asked to add the final consonant sound and to say the whole word.

Stevenson's program is comprehensive and extends through all grades. She claims to have even had success with a forty-four-year-old suffering from dyslexia. The pupils move through the program at their own pace, and they are not evaluated by comparison with others. When they have mastered a specific task, they move on to the next one.

Stevenson uses practical learning aids that tend to make learning to read fun. She calls some words "peanut butter and jelly sandwich" words and others "layer cake" words. The "layer cake" words begin with a consonant, followed by a vowel, another consonant, and another vowel. The "peanut butter and jelly" words consist of a consonant (which can be visualized as a slice of bread), a long vowel (crunchy peanut butter, so you can hear it when you eat it), a silent vowel (jelly), and another consonant (the bottom slice of bread).

Many children become confused with the letters *d* and *b*. This is true of dyslexic and non-dyslexic children. Again, Stevenson uses an easy to remember picture approach to solving this perceptual difficulty. To help the children learn the correct way to make a *d* she draws a little duck figure around the *d* for duck. She does the same thing for the letter *b,* only this time she draws a bat and a ball around the letter *b.*

These visual reinforcements enhance the child's ability to perceive and remember how the letters are formed. Stevenson has children use a large-print typewriter to "anchor words in their minds." This ensures that children will not print their letters backwards or upside down. The typewriter and computer printer are valuable tools for the motor-impaired child. They are also useful tools for the child whose penmanship is a major problem.

Many students with visual memory problems learn to compensate for this difficulty. Some teachers use songs to help children with learning disabilities memorize facts. These students learn different compensatory devices to help them remember what they have learned. Hands-on experience helps students who have trouble learning from text books. These students are tested orally because they can't express themselves by writing. This may be controversial, but it works.

I have used instructional cassette tapes for years. My tape recorder can be set to go on some time during the night when I am fast asleep. The softly playing tape always begins with the words "You will continue to sleep, but let the message become part of your memories." My taped instructions are usually placed on endless tape loops made by the Automated Learning Company of Fairfield, New Jersey, although ordinary cassettes work just as well except for the noise they sometimes make when they come to an end.

Most modern classrooms are equipped with audio-visual equipment for the children to operate. These are especially important for learning-challenged children. Programmed material allows them to progress up a ladder of difficulty according to their ability. Some college students tape their professors' lectures to play back.

Children with learning problems benefit by drilling upon facts over and over again, but the drill can be enlivened through the use of word and number games. As valuable as computers are, they don't belong in an elementary classroom until after the children have learned all the number facts and acquired a good oral and reading vocabulary.

Zelda Griffin is an innovative teacher who believes that a child's preschool years are fertile educational years and are often neglected by parents. She goes so far as to label the time between birth and school age as the "wasted receptive years." She stresses that a normal child is receptive from the moment of birth, seeing, hearing, smelling, and responding to stimuli. The child's world expands as faces, voices, and tones become familiar. Children are ready to learn. When parents notice that their small child can tell the difference between a cow and a horse by observing the difference in shape and the presence of a mane or udder, they should realize that the child is perceiving and differentiating. When a child can recite, "Jack and Jill went up the hill," parents should realize that the child could just as easily recite, "In fourteen hundred and ninety-two, Columbus sailed the ocean blue."

From birth onward, Griffin stresses that infants should be shown letters and numbers, as well as animals and pictures of things. For instance, she maintains that the statements "This is a cow; the cow says moo," and "This is an 8; it tells how many," can both be learned with equal ease. Before a child starts school, he should know the alphabet song, recognize letters and numbers, and understand the concept of 1 + 1 and 2 - 1. Some children with learning disabilities will still be able to read a little and do simple arithmetic, usually with numbers under 10.

When starting school with this knowledge, the learning-challenged child will profit. The most beneficial and important time for a parent to contribute can be found in these early years of infancy.

How do you use this receptive time?

You can begin with a formula Griffin calls SEED, which stands for Simplification, Exposure, Education, and Discipline.

Simplification: Look at and explain things in their simplest terms.
Exposure: Expose your child to every bit of knowledge you can.
Education: Tell the child as many facts as you can, and do this with enthusiasm.
Discipline: Use imperceptible training to develop correct thinking habits.

We develop the SEED of knowledge by planting and nurturing it. Start with the young infant using the three "R's" of rhythm, rhyme, and repetition. As you rock your baby in a chair, in your arms, in a carriage or cradle, he will feel the rhythm. As you sing or speak to the baby, you will use rhyme. *Mama, dada,* and *doggie* are all words that can be easily made into rhyming songs. Repetition is the act of doing and saying the same things over and over again. Your baby will be delighted to recognize something done or heard before. It is familiar; it is something the child has *learned.*

All three of these things are epitomized in the following phonetic song, which will expose your child to reading.

B, A, Bay,
B, E, Bee,
B, I, Billy-Bye, B, O, Bo,
Billy-Bye Bo, B, U, Boo,
Billy-Bye, Bo, Boo.

This little song can be used with all the consonants, and it can be used on into the toddler years. Other things you can do—as you sing the alphabet song—include holding up letters when diapering the child or when it is in the crib. Say, "Here is your *S*" or "Here is your *O*." These two letters are the easiest with which to begin. Expose the child to the letters, but don't force attention to them. Tell the child, "An *O* is a circle, a nothing. Your mouth can make an *O*." Point out things. Tell the child what everything is. Remember, it's all new to the child. You can rediscover things all over again. Count the child's fingers and toes everyday. You can also say, as you hand a child two cookies, "Here are *two* cookies for you." Be sure to mention colors, "I am putting on your *blue* shirt."

When your baby is able to walk with you, stop and point out the signs. A stop sign is a marvelous one to point out, as are the Coca-Cola and McDonald's signs. Show the child how letters are made with sticks, *O*'s, bumps, and mountains. An *A* becomes a sharp mountain with a stick across it. An *H* becomes two sticks side by side with another stick laid across them. An *M* is made with two bumps. You can show your child how to make letters in sand boxes, with chalk on concrete, or on paper or a blackboard. The words "OH" and "HOT" will be easy for your young child to learn.

Magnetic letters and map puzzles may be introduced to children when they are between the ages of two and four. They can also learn to play with real dominoes. You use a calendar to introduce a child to the days, weeks, months, and the date. If you will sing or chant these things to a child, the child will join you.

One of the best teaching aids can be a child's swing set. As you swing the child, you can develop a pattern and count the swings, one by one up to a hundred. Later, you can count by fives and tens. As the child swings, you may choose to count the planets, or the days of the week, the months, and so on. This is a good time to introduce the "B, A, Bay" rhyme mentioned earlier. Let the child suggest what to swing to: days, weeks, numbers, presidents, and so on.

Expose your children to things, but never *push* them. Ask

your child, "Do *you* want to say it, or should I?" Never insist, and be sure to stop when the child tires of the game. Always let it be a matter of the *child's* choice, not yours. Be as exciting as you possibly can. Look at everything with enthusiasm, and the child will do the same. Be curious about things: "Look at this. What do you suppose it is? Is it a worm? Yes, it is, and it lives under the earth to break up the soil for us. See, it doesn't have any legs, so it crawls along by moving its segments. A segment is a part."

None of us can ensure our children's happiness or assure them an easy transit through life. But we can prepare them for the world by giving them curiosity, the desire to obtain knowledge, and the ability to read. We can provide our children a head start in their lifelong pursuits of education by properly using their formative years.

The Mind

The mind of man is as mysterious as the universe itself and, like the universe, it is constantly being probed by experimental science. Science has shed new light on the mental processes, the emotions and behaviors. But, in spite of all this, man still wonders, "What is the mind?" We have learned much about its anatomical structure, but its mysteries remain.

We know that the brain is the large or pivotal part of man's central nervous system and that it is connected to every part of the body by a huge network of nerve cells. We know that electrical impulses race along this network at speeds of two to three hundred miles per hour. This network of intelligence controls the beating of the heart, inflation of the lungs, and the metabolism of the entire body. It coordinates the senses, stores memories, calls up memories, creates and acts upon emotions, and generates thoughts. There are an estimated ten billion gray and white nerve cells in the bumpy mass called the brain. Scientists have separated the brain into divisions, with each division relating to specific sensory and motor functions. The entire mass is integrated into one functioning unit, but each area can be identified with specific functions.

The adult brain is motionless. It does not divide, grow, or contract. Yet, in spite of its apparent inactivity, it does use about 25 percent of the body's blood supply. The brain, which consists of only 2 percent of the body's weight, is constantly bathed in blood. If there is just a fifteen-second interruption of this stream, the individual loses consciousness. Just four minutes without blood irreversibly damages the brain. An enormous amount of energy is needed for mental activity, but how this is done we do not as yet understand. The brain is delicate and swathed with unusual protection. Blood is supplied by four arteries so that, if one or two are blocked, the blood is rerouted through the remaining ones. The brain has three protective layers. No other organ in the body has this much protection. It swims in a fluid that protects it from shocks. It is encased in a tough membrane, and it is surrounded by skull bones.

The mind functions as the central part of the nervous system. When any event occurs among the cells of the nervous tissue, a variety of responses take place. There is a response to every sensory stimuli. Some of these responses are involuntary; others are voluntary. There can be both conscious and unconscious thinking responses to every sensory stimuli.

All nerve cells are similar in nature, with each one having three components: a cell body, fibers called dendrites that pick up the electrical impulses from other cells, and a single fiber called an axon which passes the impulses on to other cells. Nerve cells are essentially chemical substances designed to conduct electrical impulses.

The nervous system is made up of three structures: the brain, the spinal cord, and a network of nerves that extend throughout the body. There are three main parts of the brain: the stem, the cerebellum, and the cerebrum. There are subdivisions to these three main parts.

The cerebellum is the second largest part of the brain. It coordinates all the muscular actions initiated by the cerebrum. It controls muscular movements by contracting and relaxing the muscles so that they work as a coordinated unit. Injury to the cerebellum affects muscular coordination and the individual's ability to perform skilled activities.

The cerebrum is the largest part of the brain and consists of two hemispheres separated by a groove, yet joined together by a band of nerve tissues. The cerebrum is divided into smaller parts. Each hemisphere controls muscles on the opposite side of the body. The sensory areas of the cortex control sensations of touch, pressure, heat, cold, position, and pain. Injury to this section may cause blindness or auditory and olfactory disorders. The cortex integrates messages from the eyes and ears. The cerebral cortex is a message center that coordinates the thoughts and memories that enable the person to make decisions and store thoughts. Fears, emotional reactions, anger, and sexual urges stem from the limbic system.

The cortex not only controls the motor and sensory areas, but also plays an important part in coordinating the mental functions: memory, learning, emotions, understanding, and judgment. An injury to the left inferior frontal fold may cause aphasia (loss of the ability to understand, to speak or to write words).

Information is taken in through the senses, processed, and stored to be reproduced orally or visually. This step is physical and is therefore called a *motor* step.

There is a vast difference between the visual perceptions of adults and those of children. As children develop, they are expected to gain adult perceptions. This is a part of "growing up."

Children who have visual perception motor deficits often reverse letters and say or write *was* for *saw, on* for *no,* and so on.

In many instances, their eyes have traveled too quickly along the lines in reading. They then have to swing their eyes back to make sure of what they have read. As their eyes move backward, they sometimes read words backward and make these mistakes. *Now* is a word that can be sensible backward or forward. It becomes *won* when read from right to left. There are many words similar to this one.

Here is a way to help your learning-challenged child overcome this problem:

1. Take a ruler and beat time as your child reads from a book. Say, "One, two, ready, begin," and then have the child read the words according to your beats. If the child makes mistakes, don't stop. Have the child continue until the line has been read, and then discuss the mistakes. Assure the child constantly that everyone makes mistakes. Continue the exercise, but increase the speed as the child improves. Be sure to tell your child, "Don't look back if you make a mistake."

2. Prepare a list of words that do not tell a story and have your child read the list as you beat out the rhythm. For example:

tell was here saw north sharp boy girl they will stop old
dog cat barn pill bill red tall spot top the car ant pan car

Watch your children's eyes and be sure to keep them moving from left to right as they read.

3. When your child is ready, move on to simple sentences and continue to watch the eyes and to beat out the time for each word read. Continue this exercise until all your sentences can be read without making any mistakes. Examples:
Who will tell the boy?
Do you know where he lives?
My dad has a new car.

My dog likes to dig in the yard.
She did not feel well today.
I gave the dog a bath.
I like to play with my new ball.
Can you come to my house?
My mother likes to cook.
I like to read.

4. Have your child write those words that cause trouble and then help to analyze them. Then use those words in sentences that the child composes.

Some children have trouble with arithmetic simply because they don't line up their numbers properly. The place value is often askew. Teach your child the value of margins. It may help to use a ruler and put a box around each arithmetic problem.

Visual acuity is an educational term referring to how well people see. What they see is called *visual perception.*

Parents need to observe their child's visual efforts before their child reaches the age of three years. Do children cock their heads to one side while watching television? Do they lose their places while reading? Are they especially irritable when examining a printed page? If the answer to any of these questions is "yes," then the child should be examined by a medical eye doctor. Unfortunately, children do not "grow out of" eye problems.

Amblyopia is a medical term for an anatomically healthy eye that has not learned to see properly because of an uncorrected defect. The common name for this is "lazy eye," which is the result of the brain failing to get an interpretable signal to the eyes. Children with learning disabilities who have this problem are especially taxed.

A competent eye doctor can determine with a few simple tests whether each eye is seeing what it should. If amblyopia is found, the doctor may prescribe corrective glasses that can be readily worn, even by a three-year-old child.

Here are some exercises that can help your children improve visual acuity. Have your children examine the first word on each line, then ask them to locate one just like the first:

1. *toy*   hog, boy, coy, cow, tot, soy, toy
2. *bog*   fog, fob, tog, god, bog, hog, dog
3. *boy*   toy, coy, dog, sow, joy, boy, hog
4. *saw*   sew, son, was, saw, say, sam, sue
5. *the*   tail, tile, the, toy, till, law, tom
6. *place*   palace, parcel, please, parcel, place
7. *grill*   glair, grill, girl, green, greet, girly
8. *won*   win, own, now, won, want, wore, will, wall
9. *even*   ever, every, even, eve, elve, evil, elter
10. *farm*   friend, force, frost, farm, forest, follow
11. *twinkle*   twilight, thistle, twinkle, twinger, tickle
12. *dentist*   evident, dental, diller, dentist, dingle
13. *brown*   drown, round, brown, ground, drowned
14. *felt*   left, fine, fled, self, felt, filt, finn
15. *spot*   stop, shop, tops, spot, strop, prop, stops
16. *tub*   dub, dun, bud, tom, bud, pub, tub, ton, tit
17. *file*   life, flite, lite, line, fly, flie, file
18. *from*   form, farm, frown, forms, from, fried, frill
19. *live*   fife, live, leak, lite, life, line, like
20. *thank*   think, thick, thin, thought, thing, thank, twin
21. *grant*   greet, grin, grunt, grant, grate, grill, grite
22. *shred*   should, shall, shred, shrill, shrimp, shrine
23. *nail*   mail, male, meal, nail, nine, mine, night, nite
24. *form*   from, fill, frame, foam, form, find, friend

Additional exercises to train the eyes:

1. Have your children look around the room and count the things they see. Be sure to have them look from left to right. Don't let them back up. If they lose count, have them finish, then let them start again.

2. Have your children look out the window and count the number of things they see. Make sure that they look from left to right. Their memories will improve as they learn to recall the things they see looking *from left to right* in the room and out of the windows. They can count the trees, the plants, stones, automobiles, and so on. There are always things for them to count, left to right.

3. Have your children count the words in the sentences of books, magazines, and newspapers, always going from left to right.

4. Have your children look at newspaper cartoons, picture books, anything, for things to count.

5. Draw a line going from left to right on a paper and make sure that your children's eyes follow the line you are drawing. Let the children draw some lines of their own. Their eyes will have to follow their own lines, just make sure that they draw them from left to right.

Auditory acuity refers to how well we hear things. A problem in this area is not considered a learning disability, but it can easily contribute to one. It is very important to ascertain whether a child with a learning disability also has a hearing or other physical problem which compounds—or has even created—the child's learning difficulties.

Here are some exercises that you can use to help your child distinguish the differences in words (auditory acuity).

1. Stand about twenty feet behind your child, so that the child cannot see you. Place yourself squarely behind the middle of the child's back, so that one of the child's ears will not be closer to you than the other one. Then call out the following words. Have the child tell you which time the words are the same, and, when they differ, in what way.

1.   stair   star

2.	bell	bell
3.	what	where
4.	star	star
5.	mouth	south
6.	whose	whom
7.	south	south
8.	mountain	fountain
9.	met	pet
10.	pet	peck
11.	fly	fly
12.	black	lack
13.	brown	drown
14.	spot	stop
15.	father	father
16.	wharf	war
17.	whose	choose
18.	choose	choose
19.	come	sum
20.	whose	whose
21.	house	horse
22.	top	stop
23.	what	what
24.	wash	watch
25.	live	five
26.	pock	pluck
27.	want	what
28.	mother	other
29.	pick	pick
30.	with	which
31.	grill	will
32.	main	man
33.	water	potter
34.	two	two
35.	temper	tender

36.	wander	wonder
37.	ruffle	duffle
38.	muscle	buscle
39.	duffle	muscle

Speech articulation indicates clearness and fluency of a pupil's speech. Stuttering, stammering, slurring and plain carelessness with speaking habits are facets of articulation.

Teach your child to pronounce words distinctly.

Some children with learning disabilities fail to recognize the small differences in the sounds of words. This is especially true for many boys with learning problems under the age of nine. You can train them to speak carefully as they listen to your careful enunciation.

Read these words to your child and be sure to pronounce each one as though you were a television announcer:

mother	father	crook	rook	wheat	seat
mistletoe	collar	robber	where	there	wear
gold	cold	sold	told	fold	hold
bold	felt	tilt	silt	ride	bride
school	rule	road	rhyme	bake	cake
baker	wake	take	elephant	mechanic	machine
bleak	weak	seek	tea	see	seen
where	wear	we're	weird	wealth	health
porter	reporter	report	sort	worse	worsen
wheat	win	there	where	bleak	blend
seam	steam	stream	magic	tragic	trend
blame	shame	tame	name	claim	frame

bake	baker	wake	waken	crown	cloud
cream	clown	wound	round	sound	town
mist	mystery	miss	whist	sis	mistletoe
sense	census	where	wear	wealthy	weird
red	read	reader	radar	ever	rule
big	did	dig	din	dog	dine
even	seven	Steven	tin	tiny	thin
win	toe	go	row	sow	sin
cents	sense	rinse	ring	ting	gin

Teach your children to pay close attention by speaking to them silently. Prepare lists containing the following words as well as others with which your child is familiar. Point to a list and say, "I am going to silently say a word from this list, but you are going to have to watch my mouth to find out what word it is because I am not even going to whisper it." You will, of course, need to open your mouth wide and use your lips and tongue.

1	2	3	4	5	6
run	tub	time	caught	whip	start
ran	time	win	taught	sin	part
tan	rhyme	tin	bought	will	wart
can	whine	tom	ought	till	cart

Listen to your children read or speak and, if they are careless about endings of words, have them practice the following and other appropriate words:

love, lover, loving, loved, loves
say, saying, says, said

help, helpful, helping, helper, helps, helped
spend, spending, spender, spent
happen, happens, happening, happened
mistake, mistaking, mistaken, mistakes
place, placing, placed, placer
miss, missing, miss, missed, misses
ruler, ruled, ruling, rule, rules
clean, cleaner, cleans, cleaning, cleaned
mine, mining, miner, mines, mined
fail, fails, failing, failed

I am always dismayed when I listen to high school and even college graduates carelessly speak the final consonants or add syllables that don't belong.

Listen to your learning-challenged child pronounce the following words:

kitchen (not kitch-in) ask (not axe)   arithmetic (not 'rithmetic)
writing (not writin')   elm (not el-em)   film (not fil-em)
playing (not playin') winning (not winnin') running (not runnin')
history (not hist'ry)   ringing (not ringin')   around (not aroun')
singing (not singin')   hanger (not hang-ger) test (not tes')
geography (not jography)   disturb (watch for the final *b* sound)

Listen to your child pronounce the following words:

disturbance	athlete	garage	turning	afraid
oil	empty	cataract	depth	axle
caramel	engine	thirty	messenger	long
third	girl	bird	town	peep

There may be other carelessly pronounced words that you can hear as you work with your child.

Language processing is involved in every aspect of instruction. Often, *auditory perception* will be at the root of a problem. Children with learning disabilities often have problems following directions. They get the wrong homework assignment; they appear not to have paid attention to their teacher. This may not be true. Some children cannot sort out a teacher's voice from the other sounds going on in the classroom. Any child who is partially deaf in one or both ears, or suffers from a cold, may not be able to distinguish parts of speech. Most schools, and certainly all hospitals, possess audiometers to measure hearing problems. Some children who have suffered frequent colds, malnutrition, and past childhood diseases may possess speech defects, organic, or other functional problems. They may be labeled "retarded" simply because they are not physically strong enough to concentrate on the learning tasks. All children who are behind or have difficulty with learning skills should be physically examined.

Here are some things that you can do to help a child with auditory perception problems:

- If the child has hearing problems, a physician specializing in hearing disorders should be consulted.
- Petition the school to seat your child in a classroom position from which the teacher will be more apt to be heard.

A child who does not volunteer to answer questions in class may simply have a limited vocabulary, a handicap which will make it hard to gather thoughts and express them vocally. Often, the child may be assumed to be backward, a fact that is not necessarily true.

There are several things a parent can do to help:

1. Increase the child's vocabulary.

a. Have your children read aloud from books below their grade level. Every time they come to an unfamiliar word, write it down. Continue until you find five unfamiliar words, then teach those five words. Copy them onto another sheet of paper.

b. Continue this exercise the next day, looking for five more troublesome words. Be sure to review the previous day's words.

c. Every time your child correctly reviews a word, put a check beside it. When there are five correct responses, give the child a reward.

2. Working with children who had trouble remembering and spelling certain words, Dr. Grace Fernald wrote the words in especially large print, so that the children could trace them with their fingers until they could remember them.

a. Write the words that trouble your child in a notebook for him to review.

3. Have your child become a "detective," looking for words you call out on different pages of books. If the words cannot be found in a reasonable amount of time, point them out and mention them again later. See how quickly each word that you call out can be found. Hopefully, try to arrange for the child to find them all.

4. Help your child write a play for the two of you to perform. Read the play with expression and try to imitate the voices of the characters. For example:

Old Man: When I was a child, I had to cut wood for the
    stove and pump water from the well for the kitchen.
Child: Did you have to go to school, too?
Old Man: Yes! I had to walk five miles to get to school and
    then another five miles to get home again.
Child: Now the kids who live only a mile away get to ride a
    bus to school.
Old Woman: I had to run errands and find eggs that our hens
    had laid when I got home from school.

5. Most of your children's reading books are full of stories, which they should read with expression. Ask them to imagine how they would feel if they were the children in the stories. The purpose of this is to keep them from just reading words and put drama into their recitations.

6. Your child may enjoy playing "Radio Announcer," and should write the dialogue. For example:

> "I want to tell you about a wonderful new product called *Wammo Soap*. This soap will clean anything, and you don't have to use hot water. Your children will love it because it makes pretty bubbles when they wash their hands and face. Mothers will like it because the children will be so clean. You can get this soap for only fifty cents a bar at any store."

7. Your children may enjoy pretending they are policemen busy answering a call. Help them write the dialogue for them to read. For example:

Chief of Police: Calling car number 25. Do you hear me?
Police Officer: This is car 25. What do you want?
Chief of Police: Go to the corner of Elm Street and Main
    Street and investigate a fire.
Police Officer: This is car 25. I am on my way.

Some children with learning disabilities cannot write stories well enough for others to understand. These children do not turn in written assignments; they do not know how to use grammar properly; they leave subjects out of their sentences and get them out of order; they do not understand syntax.

There are ways in which parents can help:

1. Using the technique suggested for increasing a vocabulary, have your learning-challenged children write the words they have misspelled. Discuss them and place them in an envelope. From time to time, the child should remove the words and write them several times, using the Fernald technique of tracing over them on paper and in the air. Every time your child spells a word correctly, put a check beside the word. When the child achieves five checks, reward the achievement.

2. Teach you child how to outline writing assignments. This will help children organize their thoughts. Later, they will learn to fill in their outlines and construct their own stories.

a. Ask the child to think about what she is going to say.

b. Have her jot down her thoughts with only a word or two, but in the order that she will later write.

c. Have the child fill in the outline with complete sentences.

Memory

Your children's visual memories affect their ability to store and to recall past events which they must do if they are to put them on paper or recite them.

Here are some things which will help children with learning disabilities to improve their visual memories:

1. Have them examine a book that has a Table of Contents.

a. Have them locate something in the Table that they would like to read and list the page numbers.

b. If there is an Index, have them locate things of interest and write down the numbers of the pages indicated.

c. Have them look up these pages and read them. When they have finished, ask them to recall the information they have just looked up.

d. Have them follow the same procedure with the List of Illustrations, if there is one.

2. Pretend that the following story appeared in the newspaper:

BOY HERO

John Smith, a ten-year-old boy of Boston, Massachusetts, was playing in his front yard when he heard a scream. He looked up and saw a woman looking at a small child about to run into the street. John ran to the child in time to catch him just before he ran in front of a large truck. John held the child until the woman, who turned out to be the child's mother, was able to take charge of her young son.

Have your learning-challenged children read this "newspaper article" and then ask about it. For each item the children remember, give them a star, but, for each time a child fails to remember, subtract a star. Have them reread the article until they remember every fact.

Do the same thing for the following "newspaper article."

Yesterday, a twelve-year-old Boston boy was seriously wounded when his friend accidentally shot him with a small handgun. The boy, whose name is being withheld because of his age, was taken to the Boston City Hospital, where his condition is considered serious. The boys were playing with a gun which they did not know was loaded and belonged to one of their fathers.

You will find articles in your local newspaper suitable for your child to examine. Cut them out and use them for additional memory work.

One of the most important factors in the development in the intellectual growth of not only learning-challenged but all children is their inquisitive and persistent questioning. Parents, relatives, and teachers are often too busy to answer these questions and occasionally become annoyed. Great pains should be taken to explain everything—not to get rid of children, but to *instruct* them.

The continuous string of questions asked by children affords opportunities to explain some important truth or to teach some valuable lesson. When queried, a parent or teacher should ask, "What do you think?" Children should be listened to and have their questions answered correctly. For an older child, the teacher or parent might supply the number of the page in a book that has the answer and then have the child find it.

Every faculty can be cultivated and improved. Children with learning disabilities should be taught to think for themselves and try to answer their own questions. When several similar questions are asked and the correct answers found, encourage your children to put them all together and recall the answers. Then, let them think, judge, and act for themselves. Don't worry about their coming to incorrect conclusions.

Have you observed the intellectual manifestations of a child under eight years? What happens to the intellects of children and their reasoning powers when they are stifled by the inability or refusal of parents to answer their inquiring minds and to help feed their developing intellects? Their intellectual powers *shrivel*. They can develop a fatal dislike of books engendered by the deadly instructions of some teachers and the threat of punishment from their parents.

Before they are of school age, take time to tell your children stories, show them the operations of nature, do experiments with them, answer their questions, as well as lead them from the facts to the laws. Teach them to do their own thinking, to harmonize with the nature of their minds.

In particular, show them things that *interest* them, making ordinary things exciting and thereby stimulating, improving, and invigorating their minds.

Some children do well in school. They learn quickly and remember facts. Others, especially those with learning disabilities, often do not. Many of these youngsters have trouble paying attention. Their grades are poor. Yet they may be just as intelligent as their more successful classmates. Why is this so? It may be that their *way of learning*—their attitudes and their behavior—has affected their success in school. It may be that they need more parental help.

Successful students behave in certain ways. They have the right attitudes. In other words, they are motivated, they pay attention, they are relaxed, and they ignore distractions that might interfere with learning. Also, when they need help with their school work, they know how to get it. These things are not inborn, but they can be learned. And you can help a child with learning disabilities to gain and use them.

There are four ways to do this:

1. *Teach your learning-challenged child to pay attention.* Teach your children to use *self-talk* and *positive images*. Teach them words and phrases to help control their attention. Tell them to keep their eyes on the blackboard while the teacher is writing on it to explain a problem and their ears tuned to what she says. Help them to practice *self-talk* at home in various situations: when playing a game, helping around the house, or working at a hobby.

Tell your children to avoid negative thinking such as "It's hopeless." Rather, teach them to be positive about themselves, to say, "I can do it." Positive self-help includes the old saying "Quitters never win, and winners never quit."

• *Set specific goals with your child.* Ask your child to study lessons until he can tell you the main point of a paragraph, solve a specific mathematics problem, or repeat specific names, dates, and places mentioned in the text. Discuss each goal. Remember that many small goals—one after another—are better than a single large one.

2. *Keep your learning-challenged child interested.* Learning is a joint effort. Everyone—student, teacher, and parent—must help if students with learning disabilities are to learn. But students must realize that no one else can do their learning for them. Children must *believe* that the hours they spend studying and the effort they put into learning mean the difference between success and failure.

Reward your learning-challenged children for improvement. Your praise is music to their ears. Consider giving them special treats, trips, or privileges for special achievements. Continue to stress the benefits of doing well in school. Let them see that some benefits are immediate, such as having more free time, and that some benefits are long-term, such as earning a scholarship or an interesting job.

3. *Help your learning-challenged child to remember.* Success is not determined just by intelligence, but by the *strategies* a person uses to master facts and ideas. Understanding a subject doesn't just happen; it takes work. It takes an interest in the subject. New information must be related to familiar information.

Here are the strategies:

• *Make inferences.* Encourage your children to draw conclusions from the material they are reading. For instance, when they are reading about an invention, such as the telephone, they should consider what people would do without telephones.

• *Build bridges.* Encourage your children to build a bridge between new information and the things they already know. They should look for similarities between the new and the familiar. For example, if they are studying the court system, they could relate the judge's role in settling disputes to their own experiences with arguments and disagreements.

• *Find the main ideas.* As your children listen and read, they should frequently ask themselves, "What is the point being made here?" By constantly looking for the main idea, they must concentrate on learning the important material. This helps them to keep actively engaged in studying.

• *Categorize information.* School activities usually involve learning and remembering large amounts of information. Sometimes there are long lists of names and dates. When there are many items of information to learn, the child should group them in categories. The child should do this in all subjects.

4. *Help your learning-challenged child study.* All children, but especially learning-challenged children, need a place to study. Whether they live in a one-room apartment or a sprawling ranch house, children need study areas. It may be a desk or the kitchen table, but it must be fairly quiet and well lit.

Your child also needs a *time* for studying. Help set up a schedule for chores, work, fun, and study on a weekly basis. The schedule should be flexible enough to allow trade-offs and shifts when necessary.

• *Preview material.* Help your child begin an assignment by previewing the material—for example, by reading the introduction to a chapter, the headings, and the summary. You may have to point these out. This is like looking at a road map: your doing this will help the child create a mental "map" of what is ahead and can complete the details when the chapter is read.

• *Read and think.* When reading the chapter, your child should try to fit in the details of the mental map. This is the time to use attention-grabbing strategies—self-talk, positive images and questions.

It will help the children to pause and test their understanding of each section before going on to the next section. They should ask themselves, "What conclusions can I draw from this? How should I categorize the information? Do I see analogies? What are the main ideas?"

• *Take notes.* Very few of us can remember everything we read. It helps to take notes. These notes serve as a summary of the most important points. Your child's writing and reviewing them will help your child understand, categorize, and remember. The notes—or, for an older child, an outline—will help prepare your child for future tests.

• *Self-tests.* Your children should test themselves to see what they know and what they do not know. Show them how to make up tests on the material they are studying. If they respond well, then help them administer these preliminary "tests." They can then apply their study time more effectively on the sections where they are weak.

CHAPTER THREE

Arithmetic

The following strategies are best for helping first-, second-, and third-graders, but they may also be useful for older children who have learning problems with arithmetic.

Many pre-schoolers are easy and confident with numbers, but some are not. In special cases, a parent can institute games so that learning-challenged children will become able to deal comfortably with situations requiring an idea of what is largest, smallest, tallest, longest, inside, outside, closest, farthest, and so on. Begin with very simple addition and subtraction by counting and looking at actual objects—apples, pencils, books. Help your child learn to correctly count to 10.

There are three essentials for a child to learn mathematics. All three can be reinforced by a parent.

1. *Understanding.* The child must understand the steps involved in working and solving a math problem. If the child's ability to solve problems is based solely on memorization without understanding, the ability won't carry over from one problem to another.

2. *Practice.* Children must practice base skills—addition, subtraction, multiplication, division, fractions, and decimals—so

that they can learn and remember them and then use them correctly.

3. *Seeing patterns.* Children need to see patterns and regularity in mathematics, and they must learn ways of organizing mathematical information. Math builds and extends simple ideas into more general concepts. Good problem-solvers have certain things in common: they are quick to understand the important features of a problem, they approach a problem with confidence, and they can transfer their learning skills from one problem to another. When they get an answer to a problem, they know whether the answer is reasonable, because they are able to estimate well.

Counting

Counting is essential for learning addition and subtraction. It becomes a detriment, however, when children rely on it too heavily—especially on finger-counting—so that they never adopt more efficient ways of doing arithmetic. Children who continue to use their fingers are always slower than the other students and can never work as many problems.

Counting is more than reciting a string of numbers. It includes matching objects and arriving at totals. Research has identified six stages that a child must go through in counting, beginning with rote counting (1, 2, 3, 4, etc.) and becoming progressively more sophisticated (for example, counting from 7 to 55 to get 44, or counting back from 12 to 3 to get 9). Following this, the child is ready for open addition problems such as $13 + ? = 19$.

To help your child develop confidence in counting, use concrete objects and examples. Drop five marbles in a jar and have the child count as you drop additional marbles in the jar: 6, 7, 8, 9, etc. Use rhymes and songs such as the one that begins "One, two, buckle my shoe. . . . "

If the child has trouble keeping a mental tally when counting from one number to another, suggest reciting the first number in a soft voice and the next numbers in a progressively louder voice.

Use familiar, repetitious situations to reinforce counting. Encourage the child to count along with the second hand as it sweeps around the clock. Count the dishes on the table. Count the number of cookies in a box, the bikes in a bike rack, the leaves on a plant. Have the child touch each object as it is counted. Arrange the objects in various positions—in lines, in rows, in circles, and randomly. This will assist the child's understanding of numbers.

Estimating and Measuring

Estimation is one of the cornerstones of mathematics. It can enrich counting, measurement, and problem-solving abilities. A child who can make a good estimate of the answer to a problem clearly understands the problem. Children who can estimate are able to reject unreasonable answers and know when they are reasonably correct.

Despite the importance of estimation, few schools stress it. Those schools that use estimation in teaching arithmetic generally don't introduce it soon enough. Yet even children in kindergarten can correctly estimate relative sizes and proportions.

You can help children with learning disabilities develop estimation skills by helping them practice rounding numbers to the nearest 1, 10, or 100. This is a strategic step in acquiring this skill. Practice estimation with your child: "How many marbles do you think are in the jar?" "Who is taller, your father or your mother?" "Which is wider, the door or the table?"

Measurement is another essential, and many children are weak in this area. You can help a child by making comparisons. Ask if the child has "too much" or "too little" of something, and if an object is "too short" or "too long." A typical comparison might be "Which will require more paper to cover, the bulletin board or the door?"

Help your child practice measuring things that are longer than the measuring instrument, such as a meter stick. Include measurements that involve fractions other than $\frac{1}{2}$. Make a floor plan of your house with your child's help. Have the child take the measurements with a tape measure while you write down the dimensions.

Time is among the things that have to be measured. Discuss time with your child rather than just "telling time": "If it takes me 45 minutes to get to work, when should I leave the house to get to the office by 9:00? When should I leave the office in order to get home by 6:30?"

Age is another measurement. Ask how old the child is in months, weeks, days, hours, and minutes.

Correcting Mistakes

Find out what kind of mistakes your learning-challenged child makes in arithmetic. Use an arithmetic book to find easier problems of the same type, and make sure your child understands simple problems before going on to the more difficult ones.

Ask your child to describe how to work a problem, step by step. Doing this may help her to identify the error. While your child is doing this, look for patterns in errors, because one misunderstanding may cause others similar to it.

If your child consistently makes a subtraction error (say, 25 - 16 = 19) and you are not sure whether this is from carelessness or from lack of understanding, use objects to work with the child. Place 25 marbles in a jar and ask the child to remove 16. Make sure that the child checks the subtraction.

A child with word problem difficulties should concentrate on the information that is essential to solving the problem. Sometimes a problem includes irrelevant information that confuses the child.

Do's

Do ask your child's teacher about the kinds of help that you, as a parent, can provide. Your role is to reinforce and help your child practice the things taught in school.

Do encourage your child to restate what a mathematical problem is all about—the information it gives and the information it asks for. Putting it in the child's words will help clarify it.

Do make sure that some of the math your child does at home includes some problem solving. "How many nickels do you have in your bank?" "How many nickels do you need for an ice cream cone?"

Do use objects that your child can touch, handle, and move. Researchers call these things "manipulatives." They can be any familiar objects such as soft toys, blocks, marbles, drinking straws, and fruit.

Do reward your child with praise for correct answers. This helps build his confidence in problem-solving.

Don'ts

Don't tell your child that some people lack ability in math. Never tell your child that you were never good in math, no matter how low your opinion is of your own skills.

Don't think that girls are not as good in math as boys!

CHAPTER FOUR

Reading and Writing

Your learning-challenged child *will* learn how to read. Whether he will read fluently is a more difficult question to answer. A parent can help a learning challenged child considerably by following some simple rules:

1. Read aloud to children.
2. Talk to them about their ideas and experiences.
3. Take them places.
4. Permit them to watch television, but place limits on viewing time.
5. Take an interest in their reading progress.

If you want your child to read well and with understanding, you must begin early to lay the proper foundation. You do not need to be a professional teacher. You do need to care and to take every opportunity to help your child learn about the written language.

◆　◆　◆

The Influence Effect

In my experience, certain things influence children's successes and interests in reading.

• *Wide knowledge.* The more knowledge learning-challenged children acquire at home, the greater their chances of becoming successful readers. Children who go on trips, walk in parks, and visit museums and zoos get good background knowledge for school reading.

• *Thoughtful discussions.* The way in which you talk to your child about things in general makes a big difference. Talking can increase her vocabulary and supply of concepts. It is not enough to ask a question. You must ask a question that causes a child to think. Thought-provoking questions stimulate the curiosity needed for success in reading.

• *Talk about events.* Encourage your child to think about past and future happenings. Don't allow conversation to focus entirely on ongoing events as, for example, the clothes the child is putting on or the food that is being eaten for dinner.

Ask your child to describe something in which you did not participate—for instance, a visit to a friend's house. This sort of questioning gives children a chance to use their memories, reflect on experience, learn to describe people and events, and tell complete stories.

Children who hold lengthy conversations at home are able to capitalize on their experiences and to construct meaning from events. This is a major part in developing not only their ability to read, but also their ability to understand what they read.

Things for You to Do

• *Read aloud.* This is the single most important thing you can do for your children. Encourage children to talk, for this will increase their power of expression. When children are young, they need to talk, as this is their only method of improving their power to explain ideas. Children are meant to be incessant talkers, but they are schooled to remain quiet. Whispering children are often punished in school. Why not also punish them for hunger, or for thinking? For these are other expressions of their great needs. Don't stop reading aloud to children after they learn to read. Reading aloud forms an important bond between you and your children.

When reading aloud, keep certain things in mind. For instance, pre-schoolers enjoy hearing the same story over and over again. Books that repeat phrases, such as *The House That Jack Built,* are special favorites. They give young children an opportunity to participate by reading the repetitive parts with you. This lets children know that they can read and that reading is fun.

Begin reading to the child when the child is a year old, or even younger. Read from simple picture books. Cardboard pages are fairly easy for a toddler to turn, and this exercise will help a child learn how to handle and care for books.

Talk to your child about the stories you read. Help identify letters and words. Discuss the meanings of the more difficult words. Share *your* favorite children's books and read them aloud. Ask your children's opinions about the stories.

Ask the kind of questions about a story that will make your child think. Avoid asking questions that can be answered with a "yes" or a "no." If you are reading a story about a dog, don't ask whether the child likes dogs, but ask which breed of dog she prefers, and why.

Let these questions carry over to other areas of your child's life. Encourage your child to discuss daily activities. If your child spent the day with the babysitter, ask what sort of things they did, and how, and why they did them. Always ask the kind of questions that require children to use their memories and reflect on their experiences. Talking about experiences helps a child learn about concepts and helps build a vocabulary. These abilities help your child to become a good reader.

Compare episodes in stories to real-life events. If you've been reading *Huckleberry Finn* to your child, discuss the friendship between Huck and Jim and compare it with your child's own friendships.

• *Materials.* Have plenty of paper, pencils, chalkboards, and crayons for your child to use in drawing and writing. Writing helps children learn the relationships between letters and sounds. If your child is too young to write with a pencil, use magnetic boards and letters.

• *Records and tapes.* At a library you can borrow records and tapes that have follow-up books for young children. These add variety to reading activities.

• *Television.* If your child likes to watch "Sesame Street," "Mister Rogers," or any other educational television program, help relate the television lesson to other situations. For example, if the show focuses on the letter *B,* have your child give examples of other words beginning with a *B.* Have your child show you a toy which begins with that letter, such as a ball or bear.

Many parents are concerned that television may adversely affect a child's reading skills. Research shows that watching for a reasonable amount of time (no more than ten hours weekly) is all right and may even help a child learn. In fact, the dramatization of a novel or an animated production of a favorite story may inspire a child to read the book or story.

• *Computers.* Many companies are developing reading programs for home computers. However, there is little solid information about the impact of computers on children's reading development. One thing of which we are certain is that placing your child in front of a computer terminal with reading software won't teach reading.

• *Scrapbooks.* Encourage your child to make a scrapbook. This activity can help a child to identify words and letters. Have a pre-schooler make an alphabet scrapbook using an old notebook or sheets of paper tied with a shoestring. The first day the child could work on *A*—apple, airplane, automobile. The following day the child could work on *B*.

An older child may enjoy keeping a scrapbook about a hobby, a favorite personality, or a sport.

• *Prepare for phonics*. Phonics is the relationship between letters and sounds. Phonics will be an important part of your child's reading lessons in the first and second grades. Label objects in the child's bedroom—clock, dresser, chair, curtain, window, bear, toy car—to help the child relate the sound of the word to the written word. Teach the child rhymes and alphabet songs. Encourage scribbling and tracing letters on paper.

• *Talk about school*. You can increase your child's reading success by helping him to look forward to school as a happy place. Always talk about school in a pleasant, positive way.

• *Monitor performance*. Keep tabs on your child's school performance and, when he goes to school, make sure that homework is done correctly. Visit teachers and observe classrooms periodically.

• *Visit the library*. Make weekly trips to the library. Show your child the variety of things to read: books on hobbies, animals, crafts, sports, and famous people. Help your child choose a book.

• *Have a reading hour*. Let your child know how important reading is by suggesting reading as a leisure-time activity, or by setting aside an established reading hour every night, perhaps just before bedtime.

• *Stay involved*. Stay interested and involved in your child's growth as a reader. Encourage your child to read to you. Praise progress. Try to give your child a feeling of "can do" confidence.

◆ ◆ ◆

Writing

Writing will be of utmost importance in your child's life. It will be important from the earliest grades to college and throughout adulthood. Even though a child has learning problems, that child will need to formulate thoughts distinctly and then organize ideas clearly.

Writing is . . .

. . . *Practical*. Most of us make lists, jot down numbers, and write notes and instructions at least occasionally.

. . . *Job-related*. Professional and white-collar workers write frequently—preparing memorandums, letters, briefing papers, sales reports, articles, research papers, and proposals. Almost all workers find it necessary to do some writing on their jobs.

. . . *Stimulating*. Writing helps to organize thoughts and present them logically and concisely.

. . . *Social*. Most of us need to write thank-you notes, invitations, and letters to friends.

. . . *Therapeutic*. It can be helpful to express feelings in writing that cannot be expressed so easily orally.

Unfortunately, many schools are unable to give children sufficient instruction in writing. There are various reasons: teachers are not trained to teach writing skills; writing classes may be too large; and it is often difficult to measure writing skills.

Studies show that the writings of most students lack clarity, coherence and organization. Only a few students are able to write persuasive essays or competent business letters. As many as one out of four have serious writing difficulties. These students say that they like writing less and less as they proceed through school.

Things You Need to Know About Writing

Writing is much more of an art than just putting words on

paper. It is a final stage in the complex process of communicating that begins with *thinking*. Writing is an especially important stage in the whole field of communication. The intent of accurate reporting is to leave no room for doubt.

One of the first means of communication for your child is through drawing. Encourage your learning-challenged child to draw and discuss these drawings. Ask questions: "What is the boy doing?" "Does the house look like ours?" "Can you tell a story about this picture?"

Most children's basic speech patterns are formed by the time they enter school. By this time, children usually speak clearly, can recognize most letters of the alphabet, and may try to print a few letters. Be sure that you show an interest in—and ask questions about—the things your child says, draws, writes, or even scribbles.

Writing well requires . . .

. . . *Clear thinking*. Children may need to refresh their memories about a past event in order to write about it.

. . . *Sufficient time*. Children may have stories in their heads but need time to think them through—and even longer to write them down. School class periods are often not long enough.

. . . *A background in reading*. Reading can stimulate children to write about their own family or their school or vacation life. If your children read good books, they will be better writers and their imaginations will develop.

. . . *A meaningful task*. A child needs meaningful, not artificial, writing tasks. Children should be given interesting topics or practical assignments.

. . . *Interest*. A child must have something to write about. Some of the reasons for writing might include sending messages, keeping records, expressing feelings, and relaying information.

. . . *Practice*. Practice is necessary for developing good writing skills.

. . . *Revising*. Students need experience in revising their work; for instance, seeing what they can do to make their meanings clearer, more descriptive, or more concise.

How You Can Help

Always remember that your goal is to make writing easier and more enjoyable for the child.

• *Provide a place, a time, and materials*. It is important for a child to have a good place to write—a desk or table with a smooth flat surface and good lighting. Encourage your child to spend time thinking about writing projects. Provide plenty of paper and things to write with, including pencils, pens, and crayons.

• *Respond*. Respond to the ideas your child expresses verbally or in writing. Make it clear that you are interested in the true function of writing, which is to convey ideas. This means focusing on what your child has written, not how it is written. It is usually wise to ignore minor errors, particularly at the beginning stages when your child is just beginning to organize ideas.

• *Don't write for the child*. Never rewrite a child's work. *Do* show the correct way, suggest improvements, and have your child redo it if necessary. Meeting a deadline, taking responsibility for the finished product, and a feeling of ownership of the work are important parts of writing well.

• *Praise*. Take a positive approach and say something good about your child's writing. Is your child's work accurate? Descriptive? Thoughtful? Interesting? Does it say something?

Things to Do

• *Make it real*. Your child needs to practice real writing. You might suggest writing letters to relatives or friends. If your child is old enough, he might enjoy corresponding with pen pals.

• *Suggest note-taking.* Encourage your child to take notes when on outings, trips, walks, boat rides, car trips, or any other event where she can describe what she sees or does.

• *Brainstorm.* Talk with your child as much as possible about his impressions, and encourage him to describe people and events to you. If the descriptions are accurate and colorful, say so.

• *Encourage the keeping of a journal.* A journal is not only excellent writing practice, but an outlet to vent feelings as well. Encourage your children to write about things that happen at school and at home, about the people they like or dislike, things they want to remember or hope to do in the future. If a child wants to share a journal with you, read the entries and discuss them, especially ideas and perceptions. Make favorable and encouraging comments.

• *Write together.* Have your child help you with your letters, even such routine ones as ordering items from advertisements or more important ones to a business firm. This is an excellent practice that will enable a child to see that writing is necessary for adults and truly useful.

• *Use games.* There are many games and puzzles that can help children increase a vocabulary and help them become more fluent in speaking and writing. Try crossword puzzles, word games, anagrams, and cryptograms. Flash cards are good, and they can be made at home.

• *Make lists.* Most children like to make lists, just as they like to count. Encourage this. It is good practice and helps them to become more organized. Lists of records, tapes, baseball cards, furniture, things to do, dates for tests, social events, and other reminders can be made.

Increasing Word Power

In *Six Weeks to Words of Power*, Dr. Wilfred Funk

dramatically explains why "it pays to increase your word power." Although written for the adult market, Funk's teaching ideas are the "stock" of teaching techniques for any good school teacher and poignantly illustrate the value of a good vocabulary. One of his research projects revealed that the salaries of both executives and their secretaries corresponded with their vocabulary development.

A parent can search the books that a child will read in the next year and see that the words are added to the child's vocabulary.

Vocabulary tests are an adjunct in grading the ability of people. They are used by personnel directors to weed out applicants; the military uses them as qualifying factors when it considers candidates for officer training; colleges utilize them as a major factor in students' applications for degree programs. There is a vocabulary aspect in almost all intelligence tests.

A recent national reading survey revealed that the reading level of most people is the seventh grade, and that most material is written for twelve- to fourteen-year-old children. If you want to help your children meet or rise above the competition, increase their vocabulary. Regrettably, most schools do not offer courses in vocabulary development. Pupils are expected to increase their vocabularies as they study their regular curriculum. The individual pupil's vocabulary is expected to grow along with that of classmates. Your child's vocabulary will do exactly that, but no better—unless you do something about it:

1. Every time your child comes across a new word, help to copy it in a "vocabulary book."
2. Write its pronunciation, together with a rhyming word.
3. Write its common meaning.
4. Note the sentence in which it was.
5. Write the word in a sentence and use it in conversation.

Remember: Words are learned by rote memory. A child will have to use every new word often.

It is impossible to present a set of words or exercises for all ages. The following is a how-to-do-it example of ten words for you to use with your learning-challenged child. It will probably be necessary for you to substitute words that are appropriate for your child.

The phrases or words are in italics. After each one are four choices, lettered *a, b, c,* and *d.* Your child's task is to select the lettered word that is nearest in meaning to the italicized phrase or word:

1. *sadness*—(*a*) pleasure. (*b*) blizzard. (*c*) grief. (*d*) bruise.
2. *joy*—(*a*) regret. (*b*) amiable. (*c*) kind. (*d*) happiness.
3. *something that hurts*—(*a*) lakes. (*b*) vexed. (*c*) fracture. (*d*) terror.
4. *afraid*—(*a*) nervous. (*b*) fearful. (*c*) burned. (*d*) satisfied.
5. *anger*—(*a*) grief. (*b*) rage. (*c*) sorrow. (*d*) fearful.
6. *a trip*—(*a*) bus. (*b*) train. (*c*) journey. (*d*) airplane.
7. *night*—(*a*) gloom. (*b*) fog. (*c*) darkness. (*d*) blizzard.
8. *agreeable*—(*a*) joyful. (*b*) morose. (*c*) pleasant. (*d*) merry.
9. *stormy*—(*a*) snowy. (*b*) mountains. (*c*) blizzard. (*d*) death.
10. *gloom*—(*a*) night. (*b*) mournful. (*c*) pine trees. (*d*) moonlight.

(Answers: 1-*c,* 2-*d,* 3-*c,* 4-*b,* 5-*b,* 6-*c,* 7-*c,* 8-*c,* 9-*c,* 10-*b*)

Have your child use the words in sentences.
1. The loss of his pet filled John with *sadness.*
2. The holiday filled his heart with *joy.*
3. A broken arm is *something that hurts.*
4. The cat was *afraid* of the dog.
5. The emotion called *anger* can be frightening.
6. Most children love to take a *trip.*

7. The sun goes down at *night*.
8. The paper boy was very *agreeable*.
9. It was a dark and *stormy* night.
10. Losing a pet can make a child *mournful*.

Read the following descriptions and have your child place one of the proper words after each one. These sentences must not appear in the same order as they were on the first two lists.
 1. The sky was dark, the wind howled, and the rain poured.
 2. The stars and the moon were shining.
 3. The children looked out of the airplane's windows.
 4. The dog bared his teeth and growled.
 5. The man smiled very pleasantly.
 6. The child was nervous when he was alone in the house.
 7. Linda fell out of the tree.
 8. John attended his grandfather's funeral.
 9. The vacation had ended and John was unhappy.
 10. Pretty flowers express happiness.
(Answers: 1-stormy, 2-night, 3-trip, 4-anger, 5-agreeable, 6-afraid, 7-something that hurts, 8-sadness, 9-gloomy, 10-joy)

These words will be paired with other words that are either the same or opposite in meaning. Your child is to tell which.

1	sadness	happiness	same/opposite
2	joy	regret	same/opposite
3	something that hurts	pain	same/opposite
4	afraid	terror	same/opposite
5	anger	amiable	same/opposite
6	trip	journey	same/opposite
7	night	darkness	same/opposite
8	agreeable	morose	same/opposite

9	stormy	blizzard	same/opposite
10	gloom	sadness	same/opposite

(Answers: 1-opposite, 2-opposite, 3-same, 4-same, 5-opposite, 6-same, 7-same, 8-opposite, 9-same, 10-same)

By now, your child should be familiar with the ten words. To make sure, see if he can fit them into the following sentences. Explain that he may have to use a different tense or form to make them fit.

1. The death of his pet filled John with _____.
2. John was full of _____ when his father returned from a business trip.
3. A broken arm is _____.
4. John was nervous and _____ when he saw the bear.
5. John's body shook with _____ when he saw the lack of justice.
6. A _____ to Boston is over two hundred miles.
7. The sun goes down at _____.
8. Billy was a pleasant and _____ kind of boy.
9. It was a dark and _____ day when school was cancelled.
10. When the trip was cancelled, John was filled with _____.

(Answers: 1-sadness, 2-joy, 3-something that hurts, 4-afraid, 5-anger, 6-trip, 7-night, 8-agreeable, 9-stormy, 10-gloom)

By now, these ten words should have become part of your child's vocabulary. You should substitute new words each week. Be sure to watch out for the slippery words that elude your child's memory. Make a list of them and review them from time to time. The more your children learn about words, the more interested they will become in new subjects. As a matter of course, they will eventually want to know what writers are writing about. The preceding exercises will help you.

Demystifying Tests and Measurements

Schools have a multitude of tests for your child. Some of them may be administered even before kindergarten. There are several reasons for this:

- To place your children in an appropriate program.
- To determine any disabilities they might have.
- To suggest a teaching style appropriate for their learning style.

After your children settle in school, they will be routinely tested, but, sometimes, the test will be for a specific purpose.

All parents should know more about the tests that their children have to take. Parents of children with learning disabilities *must know more* if they are to help their children take the tests more effectively. The terminology and objectives of some of the psychological tests can be especially tension-creating for children who have self-images of failure. Helping a child improve in test-taking techniques and avoiding test anxiety are very important goals for any parent.

Chapter 5

There are many different types of measurements. Measurement is generally an assignment of numbers to events or things according to a particular rule. A measuring instrument may be a ruler, a scale, a clock, or an average attainment. Measurements have to be organized so that people can understand what they represent. We sometimes count the number of times something happens within a set number of minutes, hours, or weeks. This is called *frequency distribution*, a count of frequencies, and is represented on a scale marked off in equal intervals. These scales may be bar graphs, curves, or a tally. Educators like to have frequencies plotted as curves to provide them with a graphic picture. There are normal curves and curves skewed to one side or the other.

Psychologists use frequency distributions, one of which illustrates as central tendency, or a *measure of variability*. *Central tendency* is an *arithmetic mean*, or, more simply put, the average. The *medium* is another central tendency; this is the middle score obtained after all the scores have been ranked from the smallest to the largest. Still another frequency distribution is the *mode*, the most frequent score. All measures of variability emphasize the center of the distribution, and, in every case, there are variables. *Standard deviation* is obtained mathematically. Generally, the variable (deviation) depends upon the number and spread of scores being plotted. One use of the standard deviation is to develop a *standard score* for a test; sometimes this is called the Z score. For those statistically minded, here is the formula for constructing a Z score:

$$Z \text{ score} = \frac{\text{score-arithmetic mean}}{\text{standard deviation}}$$

Tests and people are sometimes compared to each other by something called a *centile score*. This score is obtained by examining the percentage of scores at or below the individual's score in the total distribution of scores. The term *centile score* can be used interchangeably with another term, *percentile score.* Teachers commonly refer to a child's standing in a test as being in a "percentile."

Correlation refers to the relationship of one thing to another. It is another number word or statistical expression. Psychologists are interested in the correlation between two variables. Correlations are usually expressed by numbers between 0 and 1. The 0 expresses no correlation and the 1 expresses a perfect correlation. The Binet test of intelligence is the standard of intelligence testing; hence, most other tests of intelligence seek to obtain a high correlation with the Binet. There are several ways of expressing the way things are correlated. The most common way is by ranking them according to intervals on scales of one kind or another.

Your child can develop the ability to do well on tests. And you can help.

Ask the school. If you have a child with learning problems, it would be useful for you to know the school's policies and practices on giving standardized tests and the use of test scores. Ask your child's teacher or guidance counselor about the kinds of tests your child will take during the year, and find out the schedule for testing.

One other thing: some schools give students practice in taking tests. It especially helps to make sure that children with learning problems are familiar with directions and test format. Find out whether your child's school gives "test-taking practice" on a regular basis, or whether it will provide such practice if your child needs it. For a child with disabilities, such practice is imperative.

How to Avoid Test Anxiety

It is good to be concerned about taking a test, but it is not good to experience "test anxiety"—excessive worry about not doing well on a test. Students with learning disabilities often suffer from test anxiety, which can result in disaster for the student. Such children tend to worry about their lack of success in school generally. Their normal anxiety tends to increase when faced with a test. These youngsters worry about the future and are extremely self-critical. Because of early negative experiences, instead of feeling challenged by the prospect of success, they become fearful of failure. This makes them over-anxious about tests and their own abilities. Ultimately, they become so worked up that they feel incompetent with the subject matter and the test. It does not help to tell these children to relax, to think about something else, or to stop worrying. They cannot do it. However, there are ways to reduce the anxiety.

Beside the use of meditation therapy and sleep therapy, there are other ways to reduce your child's anxiety about tests:

• *Set up a time schedule.* Knowledge assimilation takes place over time; it can take days or even weeks. Set up a schedule on which your child can depend. Students must understand that the information to which they are being exposed must relate to what is already known. They must review new material more than once. By doing this, they will feel prepared at examination time.

• *Don't cram.* Cramming increases anxiety; anxiety interferes with clear thinking. It is better to get a good night's sleep. Rest, exercise, and eating well are as important at examination time as they are at all other times.

• *Teach your child to read directions.* Carefully practice this skill at home. Teach your child to carefully spend time reading exact directions before beginning a test. This should always be done when the teacher hands out every test. If students do not understand the directions, they should ask the teacher to explain them. Students must remember that different tests may have different directions.

• *Quickly look at the entire examination.* Teach your child to see what types of questions are included in a test (multiple choice, matching, true/false, essay) and, if possible, the number of points for each. This helps students pace themselves.

   • *In essay questions, read all the directions first.* Use the margin for noting phrases that relate to the answers. These will act as directional locators when returning to the essay.

When the Test Is Over

It is important for the parents of all children—and especially for those of learning-challenged children—to thoroughly review test results. Remember that you, as parents, can help your learning-challenged child by keeping in mind that wrong answers are not a measure of incompetence but an indication of where more study is needed. This is especially true with teacher-made tests. Students can learn from a graded exam paper; it will show where they had difficulty, and perhaps why. This is especially important for classes in which the material builds on previous material, such as in mathematics. Students who have not mastered the basics of math will be unable to work with fractions, square roots, algebra, and other problems.

Discuss your child's wrong answers on tests and homework papers. Do not be negative about mistakes. Find out why your child answered as she did. Sometimes a child misunderstands the way a question is worded or misinterprets what is being asked. The child may have known the correct answer but failed to express it effectively.

It is also important for these children to see how well they used their time on the test and whether guessing was a good idea. This can help them improve their method on the next test.

◆ ◆ ◆

Chapter 5

What Are the Characteristics of a Good Test?

A good test is *reliable* in that it consistently obtains the same results each time it is used with the same person or thing. If a test is not reliable, if it doesn't correlate well with some criteria known to be reliable, then that test instrument is useless.

A good test is *valid* in that it tests that which it is supposed to test. If the test is intended to be a test of intelligence, then it must accomplish that purpose.

Psychological Tests. People are psychologically different from each other. They have different motivations, skills, interests, personality traits, achievements, attitudes, and aptitudes. Each one of these characteristics can be tested and the differences measured. This is the major purpose of psychological testing. Children are often placed in a compatible instructional group as a result of psychological tests. Diagnostic testing provides the data for the specialized instruction offered in the special needs classes. Psychological tests guide psychologists. When psychological tests are properly used, they illustrate the weaknesses and strengths of children and adults.

Aptitude Tests. Aptitude tests point to an individual's potential as one who will profit from training for a vocation. The Flannagan Aptitude Classification Test predicts students' successes in vocations by examining their inherent mental and physical abilities. The word *ability* can be used interchangeably with *aptitude*. There are group and individual aptitude tests. A test given individually is considered to be better than one administered in a group setting.

Intelligence Tests. Intelligence tests measure general ability, or what is really a wide range of aptitudes lumped together into what we call intelligence. Intelligence tests are given to students as a predictor of success in college. Generally, a student who scores less that 110 on a valid intelligence test may not succeed in college. The first intelligence test was developed in 1905 by Alfred Binet, a French psychologist, who used it to discover those children who could best profit by attending school. Binet's test was revised in America and called the Stanford-Binet Intelligence Test. It is considered by many to be the foremost test of intelligence. The Binet is administered individually, which makes it too expensive for general use. Most school systems use group tests.

The definition of intelligence has generated controversy and considerable research. The most comprehensive research on convergent intelligence—that is, intelligence in the area of education——was probably that done in 1941 by L. L. Thurstone, who decided that seven factors contributed most to an individual's aptitude for education:

1. *Verbal Comprehension*—the ability to understand and use words.
2. *Word Fluency*—the ability to use words quickly in speech or crossword puzzles.
3. *Numbers*—the ability to solve arithmetic problems.
4. *Space*—the ability to draw a design and visualize relationships among objects.
5. *Memory*—the ability to memorize and recall.
6. *Perceptual*—the ability to grasp details and see their differences and similarities.
7. *Reasoning*—the ability to understand rules, principles, and concepts for problem solving.

Although Thurstone's concepts have endured, experts are beginning to think that real intelligence involves many skills not measured by conventional intelligence tests.

Vocational Aptitude Tests. These tests measure an individual's ability to become successful in a vocation *after* the individual has received appropriate training. Some of the better ones—such as the Flannagan Aptitude Classification Test (FACT)—permit a counselor to suggest several vocational choices that fit the individual's aptitudes. Some do little more than repeat a student's expressed interest in one or more vocations. Such tests have some value to students who know what they want to do but aren't sure if they have the inherent aptitudes.

Personality Measurements. These tests have no right or wrong answers. The individuals being tested are asked how they feel about situations and what they usually do when confronted by different circumstances. Some of these tests require simple "yes/no" answers and others require answers on scales ranging from "least" to "most." Another form of personality measurement test includes the *projective* type, such as the famous Rorschach ink-blot test. Clinicians using projective-type tests look deeper into subjects' responses to the pictures or designs to discover the meaning behind the responses.

The Intelligence Quotient (I.Q.) Test. To arrive at an I.Q. number, the subject's mental age, as determined by the test, is divided by the subject's chronological age, and then multiplied by 100. The I.Q. is expressed as one number, but psychologists accept it as being a spread of 10 points on each side of the derived number, because the subject's I.Q. is affected by his mood and health. Psychologists think of a subject's I.Q. as a range of ability.

Generally, on a Binet test, a subject is considered to be:

Retarded	when the I.Q. is	52 to 69,
Borderline	"	70 to 79,
Low-Average	"	80 to 89,
Average	"	90 to 109,
High-Average	"	110 to 119,
Superior	"	120 to 129,

Very Superior when the I.Q. is 130 to 139,

Genius " 140 and higher.

Teachers like to have their students' test scores expressed in *grade equivalents*. Publishers are aware of this and provide a table to convert the derived or standard scores into grade equivalents. A grade equivalent is expressed in years and months. A grade equivalent of 6.5 means the sixth grade plus five months. If a score was halfway through the fifth grade, a child would be doing work a year ahead of his grade placement. If another child received a score of 3.5 and was about halfway through the third grade, he would be performing at grade level. Unfortunately, tests published by different companies produce different results. One company's test may produce one grade equivalent for an individual, while another company's test will produce another score for the same subject and the same child.

What is the norm?

Before a test is offered for sale, the publisher administers it to a large number of people. The test may be changed many times before the publisher is satisfied and calculates the average scores. These scores are called *norms*, or normal scores. Later, when the test is in general use, an individual score is compared with the normal scores. The words *percentiles* and *stanines* are educational terms that, for the average individual, mean about the same thing as "normal score."

Psychologists correlate a pupil's I.Q. with achievement. For instance, if a psychologist determines that a pupil has an average or better I.Q. coupled with an achievement that is below grade placement, he knows that the child can do better. He then makes suitable recommendations to the child's parents and teachers, which may result in the child's being recommended for help in the special education department.

Many tests are used to determine specific disabilities.

Different school systems use different tests, and psychologists have their preferred ones. A partial list can be found in the Appendix, and parents should familiarize themselves with at least the general characteristics of those suggested for their learning-challenged children. But even this array of psychological tests is not exhaustive. There are hundreds of psychological tests on the market.

A word of warning and advice for the users of any test that predicts occupational success: *Determined students have always confounded psychologists and their array of psychological tests.* If you and your child are truly motivated to reach some goal, go for it. Do not let anyone, or any test, discourage you from going all the way.

It is often difficult for the average individual to obtain a psychological test. Publishers *qualify* the would-be buyer according to a set of standards: "Test purchaser must have an approved application for the purpose of these tests, on file with . . . ." Even graduate students cannot purchase them for research purposes without their professors' endorsements. However, your school or clinician can get these tests for you. For parents of learning-challenged children, familiarity with these tests can be very helpful in teaching children how to prepare for them.

CHAPTER SIX

A Psychologist's Recommendations

The following recommendations are not meant to take the place of the in-person recommendations of a professional trained to counsel children who are in serious trouble academically or socially. However, as a psychologist, it has been my experience that there is much that parents of even seriously troubled children with learning problems can do to help them change their behaviors.

You can use these commonsense recommendations just as well—and maybe better—than any professional can. After all, who knows your child better than you?

Our grandparents didn't have a plethora of psychologists to advise them or complicated rules to follow as they raised their children. They went to church, prayed for help, and used common sense in raising their children. Grandmother's principles may have been old-fashioned, but they were pretty good. They still are.

Many teachers work with children because they feel a "call" to teach that resembles a preacher's "call" to the gospel. Most teachers love to work with children. Teaching the fundamental

skills is their primary objective, but they have a secondary purpose that is just as important. Teachers help their students develop
moral values and social skills. Along with parents, they counsel
children. These responsibilities are also objectives for principals
and other school administrators.

In 1968, I added a school psychologist's credentials to my
curriculum vitae. I did this in order to better understand the emotional as well as the educational problems of the children I wanted
to help.

Children, especially those with learning disability problems,
are often misunderstood and the wrong "prescription" is applied.
If this happens, then the "prescription" won't work. More than
one "prescription" might be needed for children with learning
problems, because they may have multiple problems. I have found
it best to work with just one problem at a time; however, after re-
solving that problem, I proceed to the next one. Sometimes, secondary problems resolve themselves when the primary one has
been overcome.

Here are two preliminary considerations:

1. *Blame.* It is easy to blame someone—the child, the school,
the parents, or the peer group—for the problems of a child with
learning difficulties. Parents tend to blame themselves for their
children's problems. You should avoid making judgments, and
you should not blame yourself or someone else for your child's
problems. Review all the positive things that have been said and
done for your child. This careful review will assuage some of
your anxieties.

2. *Focusing.* Lay people tend to focus their attention upon
the symptoms of a problem instead of the causes. The solutions
should be aimed at the roots of the problems and not the symptoms. When a child tells a lie about test results, the attention
should be focused upon the reason behind the lie—not the lie itself. Children with learning disabilities lie about their failures for

a variety of reasons. An important one is their inability to deal with not meeting their parents' expectations.

Aggression

Many children with learning disabilities withdraw, but others have aggressive, hostile feelings and act in inappropriate ways. Aggression can take many forms.

Constructive aggression is a healthy self-assertiveness that preserves life, because it is based upon facts. It is usually a reaction to someone or to some threatening outside force.

Destructive aggression is not based upon facts, and it is not needed for self-defense.

Inward aggression is often found in learning- and behavioral-disabled children and adults who turn their anger inward. Such aggression can be a troublesome characteristic. Teachers and parents are often confounded by children who are extremely self-assertive, ready to fight, and who seek to dominate others, including the adults who must interact with them.

Aggression is often encouraged in our society, especially by parents and coaches who seek to inculcate this characteristic in children. It is often considered to be a normal and even desired characteristic. It is allied with competitiveness and needs to be curbed, especially when it becomes violent.

Aggressive learning-challenged children who are controlled at home sometimes act out their aggressions in school to confound their teachers. Sometimes these children get out of hand and are so disruptive they are sent home, or even *away* from home. The trouble with this is that the child may not be aware that what he is doing is wrong. He may feel justified in aggressive actions and feel that he is right, while others are wrong.

Some causes of aggressive behavior are:

- hostility that has been repressed,
- over-indulgent parents,
- poor home management,
- compensation for learning problems,
- compensation for physical problems.

There are many commonsense methods for helping learning- and behavioral-challenged children to deal with specific undesirable emotional responses. Some can be initiated by parents; others demand the attention of trained psychologists. Here are some primary considerations and suggestions.

• *Time out*. Schoolteachers frequently use the time-out procedure, and you can do the same thing at home. When your children are misbehaving, send them away from you to someplace where they will not find pleasant things to do, but don't send them to a dark closet and shut the door on them. Have them remain in seclusion until they are able to return to you and are in control of themselves.

• *Contact sports*. If your aggressive children are playing contact sports that encourage aggression, remove them from the sport. They will only get worse. They will not work out their aggressions on the playing fields. Interest them in something that does not encourage aggressive behavior. They may enjoy self-competitive sports: fishing, golf, skiing, or swimming.

When you are involved with children who have aggression problems as well as learning problems, you must reinforce their self-esteem while making sure that you do not reinforce their aggressiveness. If you send a child to a room as time out from an aggressive sport, the child must not have video or other interesting games available. In this case, they would enjoy the time out and it wouldn't work.

• *Suspension from school*. If your child is sent home from school for being overly aggressive, make sure that this suspension time is not spent at the movies, playing, or the like. Consider making the child do some work around the house: cleaning, washing, polishing, and raking. This time-out experience should be less desirable than going to school. The child should not look forward to being sent home again.

You will want to know what the trouble is at school. Especially with learning-challenged children, make sure you or their teachers are not asking them to do more than they can do.

• *Sibling aggression.* If your children cannot get along with one another, then the siblings should be kept as far apart as possible. Try to arrange separate sleeping accommodations. Teach them to respect each other's privacy and personal possessions. Reward or praise your children's acts of personal kindness to each other.

• *Excessive fighting.* Your child must understand that *both* parents disapprove of this behavior. However, you should listen and make sure the child is not the object of some neighborhood bully. Teach your child to count to ten before saying or doing anything in anger and to come home immediately when upset.

• *Aggressive behavior.* If your child enjoys making fun of others, examine your own behavior. Your child's behavior may be a duplication of your own aggressiveness or prejudice.

• *High-risk situations.* Some experts believe that the accident prone individual is especially prone to accidents because of some psychological or physical problem. A child or adult may feel guilty for having committed a sin or crime and is subconsciously punishing themselves as a form of penitence.

Your children may direct their aggressive tendencies internally, but there could be physical reasons for their accidents. In any case, they should have a medical examination before going any further. If there is nothing wrong physically, the problem may be dealt with as a psychological one. A learning-challenged child may feel guilty for some real or imagined event that happened so long ago she cannot consciously remember it. The guilt feeling may be real or imagined; the result is going to be the same.

Remove children from as many high-risk factors as possible. See that medical care is received. Keep objects of danger away from them, including kitchen knives and tools that can cause harm. If they play contact sports, shift them into an activity in which they are less likely to injure themselves. They need a psychologist to help them eliminate their guilt feelings. Don't expect them to "grow out of them," but realize they may carry them into adulthood unless they receive treatment.

• *Masochistic tendencies. Masochism* is the term given to the enjoyment of suffering from either a psychological or physical cause. It is thought to have a sexual basis. The suffering can be self-inflicted or inflicted by others. It is called "arranged" if it is consciously sought. It is a sexual perversion if it is sexually sought.

Learning-challenged children with masochistic tendencies need medical/psychological attention and, like high-risk children, should be kept away from weapons and tools that they might use to injure themselves. They should be restrained from viewing shows of a violent nature. These children need the specialized attention that can only be found in a hospital where they can be observed around the clock by specialists.

• *Suicidal threats.* If your child threatens to take his or her life, the threats should be taken seriously. You must not ignore this as being just another attention-getting device. It *is* that, of course, but the child may carry out the threat. You will find suicide prevention centers listed in the "Yellow Pages" of your telephone book. Take the child there for immediate guidance.

• *Violent behavior.* If your child is violent, there may be homicidal tendencies. Your child needs immediate professional help, before something serious happens to the child or someone else—when professional help may be ordered by a court.

If your child attempts to use a weapon upon another person, or has developed sadistic tendencies, this youngster may be seriously disturbed and needs immediate professional help.

Your seriously troubled child may need hospitalization along with professional care. Twenty-four-hour supervision that is only possible in a hospital may be required. You may not realize it, but your child may believe that there is no one at home who understands or who can be talked to about those things which are important.

Anti-Social Behavior

Anti-social behavior usually involves children's use of excessive force when seeking to get their own way. They may refuse to abide by your rules, the school's rules, and the community's rules. They may destroy or deface both public and private property.

A child may be disobedient or excessively stubborn, or even lie, cheat, or steal. This behavior can easily develop in a home where the child feels unwanted, misunderstood, or is without the freedom to develop personal interests. Sometimes, the home and the school disagree about a child's behavior, and this disagreement contributes to the child's anti-social behavior. Such children cannot always be expected to resolve their own problems if the adults in their lives can't resolve theirs. Generally, a difficult home situation will result in a child's having school problems. A child from such an environment may refuse to do homework, may not care about passing or failing, and may talk or find other ways to disrupt a class. These children may show little or no interest in learning or improving themselves, much to the dismay of teachers and parents who may not realize their contribution to the child's dilemma.

Here are some recommendations for specific anti-social behaviors which a parent can attempt:

• *Cheating*. Ask yourself, "Why do my children feel that cheating is necessary? Are they trying to live up to my expectations, but can't manage to do so? Are they worried about competing with their brothers and sisters? Are they seeking a reward for an achievement they can't honestly manage?" Talk about these things with your children. Let them know that you will love them regardless of how well they do in school.

• *Arson.* The first time a child sets a fire, it can be accidental. Children are naturally inquisitive, and matches are somewhat intriguing to them. Keep matches and all other fire-starting materials away from children. If you think that your child is intentionally starting fires, then you have an angry child who may want to get even for some real or imagined injury. This child needs professional help before something terrible happens to cause this young person to become a ward of the state. The technical name for someone who deliberately starts fires is *pyromaniac*, and the illness is called *pyromania*.

• *Forgery.* Your child may forge your name to a report card if there is fear of showing it to you. Ask yourself whether you or your child's teacher have used the report card as an instrument of intimidation. Is it going to be used to take something away from the child: activities, freedom, or some cherished object?

Be sure that your learning-challenged children understand that you know they feel badly about poor marks on their report cards and that you are sympathetic. Ask, "Is there something I can do to help you to get better marks?" Let children know that they are still worthy and good persons and more important than a report card.

• *Lying.* Children with learning problems may use lying as an unproductive way of reacting to your demands. They may lie in an attempt to make themselves look better to you. Don't overreact to their lies, but sit down and discuss them. Find out why they are lying and what they are afraid of. Children need to learn that lies hurt you more than the truth ever could.

• *Stealing.* If your child has stolen something, be sure that it is returned and paid for, even if it has been damaged or used.

Don't reward the child for returning the item, for that will only encourage stealing again. Be firm with the child. Avoid moralizing. Avoid name calling—"You are a thief!" Simply tell the child, "You must take it back, because it is not yours," and be prepared to accompany the child. If stealing continues, start removing privileges and don't return them until you are convinced that the child can be trusted not to steal. Try to find out why the child stole. Was she angry with someone and wanting to get even?

• *Truancy*. Many children with learning disabilities begin to hate school. Talk with your children and try to find out why they skipped school. Has someone made fun of them? Where did they go? Who were they with? Are they behind in their school work and discouraged about catching up? Do they need extra help?

• *Vandalism*. You want your child to grow up and become a responsible person. Help by arranging to repair any damage the child might have caused. After paying for such destructiveness, see that the child becomes involved in constructive activities, so there won't be any time left over for destructive vandalism.

• *Disobedience*. If your child is disobedient in several ways, work with the most disobedient act first, and then tackle the others. Don't expect to change this behavior overnight. Don't jump on the child for everything done wrong, but don't overlook the actions either. You may need to give a child time to think about the disobedience. Don't be satisfied with a trite "I'm sorry" for each rude act. This response becomes useless if children discover they can get away with rude acts just by saying, "I'm sorry."

Parents should agree about the manner in which they raise their children. This is especially difficult if the child has a strict father and an indulgent mother who seeks to compensate for her husband's strictness, or vice versa.

Children who are regularly disobedient may unconsciously be in the process of telling their parents something about their feelings. The parents should try to find out what it is. Is the school work too hard? Is the child testing a parent's love?

• *Carelessness*. Children need to be motivated to be careful. Parents should remember that children will place their own values upon things. The child may consider unimportant something of which parents think highly.

Are you trying to get more from your children that they are capable of delivering? If you are, your children may become careless. Try reducing your expectations.

Many children do better with their homework if they are with other people. They like to do their homework in the kitchen, where they can interact and watch their mother prepare the dinner.

• *Negativism*. Parents should not panic when their child says no to requests and suggestions. They should ignore the negative answer and include the child in things they believe are appropriate. If they reward a child for a positive reaction, the child's negative reactions will diminish.

Most children between the ages of four and eight are somewhat negative, and they should be compelled to comply with reasonable adult requests. Should the child continue with an unreasonable negativism after the eighth birthday, the parents should suspect that there is an emotional problem.

• *Running away*. The runaway child is growing up and wants more freedom than parents are willing to allow. Parents need to sit down and arrange limits that are acceptable to all parties. The child should be encouraged to talk about his concerns. The parents need to explore the factors that caused the child to run away.

Children facing their teens need professional counseling. In today's atmosphere, the next time your child runs away, you may not get him back.

• *Teasing*. Many adults like to tease each other and their children. In this manner, they set an example for their children to follow. Parents need to examine their own behavior before they criticize that of their children.

Parents with teasing children can extinguish this problem by rewarding their children for "non-teasing time." A program can be designed whereby the length of "non-teasing time" can be extended from just an hour or so up to a week. By then, the teasing problem will be under control and probably forgotten.

• *Egocentrism*. The *ego* in egocentrism refers to the "I," or the conscious self. This is considered to be the center of the human being's personality, and it is involved with daily social situations. The ego works as a mediator between the standards that the individual has to live with (the superego) and the subconscious desires that are often violent (the id). The ego is an important part of the personality and contributes to the aims of the person.

Egocentric children may be creative and so sure of their own capabilities that they ignore the opinions of others. However, an egocentric child over six years old who has not shown any unusual intellectual capabilities may be a neurotic child who is not growing up properly.

Is this child your only child? Do your family activities center on the child? If your answers to both questions are "yes," you may be contributing to a child's egocentricity. You might get your child a pet, in the hope that the pet will get her mind off herself and onto something she might be expected to love. Become involved in adult activities that don't include your child. Let her find her own lifestyles and her own friends.

• *Daydreaming*. Daydreaming can be symptomatic of a psychological problem and not just inattentiveness. When you see this symptom, try to interest your child in a physical activity. A child cannot daydream when physically involved in an activity. The idea here is to direct your child's attention away from himself.

Don't waste your time in accusations, such as "You are wasting your time in useless daydreaming." Your child sees daydreaming not as a problem, but as an attractive alternative to something else. You have to encourage your child to change.

Bright children who lack challenges tend to daydream. If this happens to your child in a classroom, the curriculum should be adjusted to provide a more stimulating environment.

A daydreaming child may be perfectly normal, gifted, or retarded. There are no intellectual restraints to daydreaming.

Have you had the children's hearing checked lately? Are they on the edge of becoming emotionally disturbed? Talk to them and find out what they are interested in doing. Keep them busy with puzzles and games and other activities that will keep them mentally occupied.

• *Isolation.* Isolated children resist becoming involved with other children. Essentially spectators, they have a passive outlook and are uninterested in the opportunities offered to them. Parents see them as being unhappy but don't know how to encourage their interaction with other children.

Home environments need to be modified to desensitize children against the factors that have isolated them. There are factors in the home lives of these children that need to be resolved.

• *Shyness.* Shy children should be encouraged to talk about themselves. You need to communicate with them. Open up discussions by asking questions, such as where they have been, what they want to do in the future, and what they like to do.

Ask them to read for you, and then ask questions about what they have just read. If a child is a "social isolate" within her classroom, try to find another child with similar problems and get them together. They may find each other non-threatening and be able to share thoughts and activities together.

Is this child excluded from your family discussions? Are some of your family discussions carried on at the child's level? Do you call attention to the child's shyness? Do you try to include the child in your conversations?

Here are some things you can do to include your children in your life: let them answer the telephone; have them take messages for you; when guests arrive at your house, have the children show them around; get some puppets and encourage your children to tell stories with the puppets doing the talking; set aside some special time every day for talking. Just being a part of the preparations for dinner can assimilate children into a family situation and provide time for conversation about their problems.

• *Perfectionism.* The perfectionist child may be *afraid* to make mistakes. Have you assured your child that it is all right to make mistakes? Did something happen in the past that was unpleasant because someone made a mistake? Have you said that you expect perfection and that you won't settle for anything else?

Don't expect your children to grow out of perfectionist traits. You can expect those traits to continue developing unless you counteract them while your children are still impressionable. Examine your own attitudes and expectations. Ask yourself whether you have set unrealistic standards that the children are attempting to reach. Make sure you are not reinforcing these perfectionist traits in some way.

• *Paranoia.* Paranoia is an uncommon neuroticism that will continue developing unless there is therapy. All other factors in a subject's personality may be perfectly normal, but if there are delusions of grandeur or of persecution present, paranoia may exist.

If you think your child is paranoid, seek examination by a professional. Your child may need the attention that can only be given at a special school. There is a possibility that the child is emotionally disturbed.

• *Withdrawal.* Try to find another child with whom your child will be comfortable. Encourage this new child to come to your home, and involve both children in play activities. Your child may feel less threatened if the new child is of a younger age.

Every time your child reaches out to someone, the effort should be encouraged and, if appropriate, rewarded.

• *Domination.* The dominating child usually is covering up a feeling of inferiority in some way by using a poor adjustment technique. The child needs a better self-concept.

• *Boastfulness.* Boastful children seek attention in an effort to cover up feelings of inferiority. They do not want anyone to discover these feelings. Do not try to discredit these boasts. Calmly ignore them and praise their real accomplishments.

Boastful children need to find real success. You can help them by involving them in activities in which you know they can excel.

• *Manipulation.* Manipulative children are, for some reason, seeking power. They will seek power not only over their peers, but over their parents and other adults as well. Usually, parents are not consistent in handling such children, who may be "operating" between the two of them. These children may have discovered that they can get their own way by pitting one parent against the other. For such children, family relationships are usually confused.

Do *not* permit your children to manipulate you. For one thing, it isn't something they really want to do. They would prefer to have positive direction coming from you. Children normally test their parents to see just how far they can go in getting their own way, but it is just a game that many of them like to play. Children's good behavior should be reinforced with praise and rewards. They need reasonable and consistent rules by which to live.

• *Over-Dependence.* Children normally want to become independent. Dependent children lack confidence, so they turn to a parent or other adult for reassurance. School is often the source of anxiety in children. If your child is behind in her lessons, her anxiety will increase. Obtain a tutor to bring the child up to grade level.

Camping is a good way to increase a child's feeling of independence. A child will be more enthusiastic about camping if accompanied by a friend.

"Wean" your children away from you by giving them ever-increasing increments of independence. You must guard against the possibility that you are somehow encouraging their dependency upon you. If you are an anxious parent, you may be passing on your anxiety to your child. Encourage your child to have friends, to play ball, to go fishing. You need to encourage your dependent child to solve her problems by giving her the freedom to do so.

• *Submissiveness.* Do you overwhelm your children? Are they afraid of you? Are they afraid of someone else? Has something happened to them? Are you over-protecting them?

Take a good look at your own anxieties. Your children need protection, but it should be low-key—always in the background. You will not always be there to protect them. They must learn to handle their own problems, and they need the rough and tumble encountered in "growing up" if they are to survive.

• *Rebellion.* Do you give in to your children when they misbehave? If you do, then you are encouraging rebellion. Your children have learned that rebellion will enable them to get their own way. Unfortunately, rebellion will not work in the world that they will someday have to face. Begin by ignoring them when they are rebellious, but, when they cooperate, give them all the quality attention they have earned. In this way, they will learn the value of cooperation.

Rebellion may be a result of a breakdown in the family relationships. In that case, family counseling may be necessary. Family members are often so closely intertwined that they are unable to comprehend their own interactions.

• *Rivalry.* Children should have some time to be alone with their parents. Each child should have an opportunity to remain alone with parents after brothers and sisters have retired. At this time, the parents should listen to that child talk about his special concerns. Every child needs to feel the closeness that can't be experienced when other siblings are present. Each child has special interests, and some of them are private.

◆　◆　◆

Any sort of physical punishment will usually produce hostility directed at the person administering the punishment. Spanking or other physical slaps are usually counter-productive. The child will want revenge.

Sexual Adjustment

Confusion in sexual identification comes early to a child and can be especially confusing to a learning-challenged child. Communication is the main focus. Answer your children's questions about sex honestly, for that will encourage them to ask more sexually oriented questions. This will help them to grow up emotionally healthy. Children do not want to hear long lectures about sex, but they will listen to and accept all the factual information they can get.

Should you discover your child masturbating, do not act in such a way to create guilt. Overreaction can result in guilt feelings that will plague a child for life. Don't try to shame such children, but do get them involved in physical activities. Keep them so busy that they won't have time for extraneous sexual activity.

Mothers should stop dressing their sons as soon as the boys are old enough to dress themselves.

Children are interested in sex and may seek to inspect each other's sexual organs. These mutual inspections should be discouraged, but not in a threatening way. Threats won't work. You can't watch your child all the time, and you wouldn't want to even if you could. The best way to handle your child's natural curiosity about sex is through frank discussion. Take the initiative, and don't leave your child's sex education up to the kids on the streets. They will—if you don't.

◆　◆　◆

Affective Behavior

Affective behavior is the technical name given to psychological problems that affect the emotions so much that overt behavior results. The most common forms of affective behavior are *phobias*.

Talk to your children about those things of which they are afraid. Be specific and positive without reverting to saying, "You are too old to be afraid of this." Such a reaction would give your child another problem: feeling guilty about being afraid. Help your children overcome their fears in small increments. Reward a child for every advance made toward self-confidence.

A general example: Is your child afraid to go swimming? Don't force him, but let him enter the water a little at a time. It may take several years for him to learn to swim. There is no hurry. Let him fish from the shore rather than from a boat. Have him approach the water gradually.

There are a few specific phobias of which a parent should be aware:

• *School Phobia.* School phobia is a common type of affective behavior, sometimes caused by dependence on the mother and other times by negative school experiences.

Do everything you can to get your children into school except by using physical force, for that would panic your children. Their fears are real and should be taken seriously. School phobia is sometimes a home-related fear. Ask yourself, "Have I kept my children so emotionally close to me that they are reflecting my own needs and fears?"

The solution may require you to go to school with your child and sit quietly in the rear of the classroom. You must not leave the room without your child's consent, even though the child may be working quietly and seemingly ignoring you. Your child knows you are there, and that's why he is working. Don't sneak out the back door. If you do, you will not be trusted again. Things will get better, and soon you will be able to say, "I want to step out for just a few minutes, and then I will be right back." Before long, you will be able to go one step farther: "I have some things that I must do at home. Will you be all right here? I will be home when you get there." Soon, you will have desensitized your child to the inevitable separation. Then you will only have to accompany your child to the school yard. It won't be long after that when he will find friends to walk to school with and school phobia will have ended.

• *Test Anxiety.* Students with learning disabilities are especially affected by their fear of failing tests, which can cripple a student's chance of getting a quality education.

Telling your learning-challenged child to try harder will only increase her anxiety. When you tell your child to try harder, you are really saying that you expect failure; therefore, that's what the child expects to do. If your child expected to succeed, there would be no need to try harder.

You need to reduce your child's anxiety about tests. Here is how to do it:

1. Make sure that your child gets another chance to take the tests that were failed. It may be the fear of tests and not the lack of knowledge that prevented the child from being successful the first time.
2. You may have to request that the teacher orally test the child, for awhile.
3. Teachers can build a child's confidence if they will only count right answers and ignore the wrong ones for awhile. A school staff will often cooperate if they believe that the child is more important than the test.
4. It may help your child to sit near a friend while taking a test. A friend gives moral support, but does not supply

the right answers.
5. Teach children relaxation techniques. If they relax physically, they will relax mentally as well.

• *Depression.* Another form of affective behavior is depression. Depression is a morbid sadness which is different from grief and is unrealistic as to what has been lost. Depressions vary in severity from a simple neurosis to a severe psychosis. Depressive problems are usually associated with body complaints.

Get children involved in action-type activities. Find special projects to interest them. Keep them so busy that they won't have time for depressive thoughts.

A depressed child is a potential suicide. The causes of depression need to be resolved immediately. Professional help may be essential.

• *Hypochondria.* Hypochondria is a neurosis primarily caused by an anxiety that has gotten out of control and become a defense mechanism. Marked by a persistent over-concern with the state of health, hypochondria entails body complaints accompanied by a demonstrable organic pathology.

You should not assume that your child is a hypochondriac without the advice of your physician. Only if the doctor cannot find something wrong can you presume that your child's complaints are psychosomatic.

Are you expecting too much of your child? If you are, then you should modify your expectations. Therapy should attempt to make children comfortable with themselves. They should feel secure of your love regardless of their accomplishments. A child will not grow out of hypochondria; you must locate the cause and remove it.

• *Inferiority.* Children with learning disabilities often feel inferior because of their learning problems. They feel unintelligent and experience other feelings of inferiority. Is your child especially small? Has the child been adopted? Have such children been devalued by their peers, their teachers, or members of the family? Are they overweight? Are they behind in their schoolwork?

Therapy begins with the idea that nobody is perfect. Praise a child for each accomplishment, but do not resort to false flattery. The child will recognize flattery for what it is worth. Talk about a child's interests. If children are behind in school work, get them a tutor. If they have been devalued because of some physical drawbacks, help them find attractive alternatives to offset their drawbacks.

• *Failure in the Thinking Process.* Tension is often the primary cause for this type of failure, although there are numerous other ones. Some children with learning disabilities develop or acquire trouble in their thought processes because of mental processes, but educational deficits often develop from poor teaching.

Emotional disturbances can create severe problems that require the services of a trained psychologist who can devise appropriate remedial programs. The remedial programs are based upon the child's strongest assets.

Troubled children often resist remedial programs and defeat the best efforts of their teachers because the programs fail to address the psychological dynamics behind the problem. All too often a child is painfully lifted from one plateau to another. If psychological problems stay with the troubled child, educational deficits will also remain.

• *Failure Due to Poor Emotional Control.* All children need some success if they are to gain control over their emotions. Children should not be criticized for all of their mistakes. That would only cause them to make more mistakes. Children with learning disabilities do not intentionally make mistakes, so a parent should constantly accentuate the positive side.

There are infinite levels of intelligence. A high level is needed for success in college. Have you determined that your children should go to college regardless of their intellectual endowment? The goals you have set for your children should be in line with their abilities.

• *Pseudo-retardation*. Children with learning disabilities sometimes act as though—and think that—they are retarded even though they are of normal intelligence. Because they often experience failure, they may enjoy the helpless feeling and even the special classes where fewer demands are placed on them. These children may be fooling themselves, their parents, and their teachers into spoon-feeding them knowledge.

If at all possible, children with learning disabilities should be in a regular classroom. Their parents need counseling because they may be inadvertently contributing to their children's problems. The child's teacher should be alerted. The children should not be allowed to act retarded if they are not. They should be encouraged to do things for themselves.

• *Fantasy*. Fantasy is an imaginary series of events or mental images, which are normal for children. This may represent the child's attempt to avoid emotional conflicts.

Fantasy is *not* imagination. Imagination is considered to be the most creative facet of the human mind. But extreme fantasy is an illogical mental flight to irrelevancy with no connection to reality. The child with a definite fantasy problem must learn to separate facts from fantasy. Bring children back to reality whenever they take off into their fantasized worlds.

If your children's fantasies are beyond their control, they need psychiatric evaluations.

• *Personality Disturbances*. Children with severe anxiety problems have little control over their impulses. Their thoughts and actions may not be coordinated and may even go in different directions.

There are different degrees of integrative behavior problems. Some of them need professional remediation. While impulses are readily identified, their origins are hard to find.

• *Impulsive Behavior*. Small things will cause impulsive children to lose control over their impulses. They are quick to strike other children and tend to disregard home and school rules. They may not do their homework and may talk out loud even after their teachers have told them to be quiet. They can't play with other children without disrupting the game. Other children may refuse to play with them. Unfortunately, these children do not realize they are doing anything wrong.

You can help these children with the reward system. This is one of my standard approaches. Make a chart listing all the goals you want to see reached, and reward the child for each step made along the way to these goals.

Some teachers subtract a few stars from the chart when the child slips backwards. This may be more effective than my method, which tends to ignore mistakes and concentrates solely upon the positive steps.

• *Blaming Others.* Take time to listen to a child's side of every story in all confrontations. After feelings have run their course, analyze what has been said and then explain why these feelings are being experienced. If you are too closely involved with the child, engage a friend to listen to the story and decide who is at fault. This is arbitration, so the rules of arbitration should be made clear before the process begins.

• *Avoidance.* Some children will try to get out of doing just about everything, including chores such as taking out the trash. If your child's avoidance techniques are consistent, you will be able to anticipate any excuses. Before asking children to do something, and before they have had a chance to express their feelings about the job, let them know that you *know* how they feel and explain why the job has to be done—and *by them.* "I know just how tired you must be, but so am I; and you are the best one to do this."

• *Denial.* If children continue to deny something after they have listened to the facts that make their denial irrational, you can be sure that they are under pressure. Find out what the pressure is and reduce it. This should be your greatest concern.

• *Compulsive Behavior.* The remediation of compulsive

behavior requires professional therapy. There isn't much that you can do to alleviate this problem other than to locate the stress that your child is under and attempt to reduce it.

• *Hallucinations.* Hallucinations are false sensory perceptions. They are false because there are no actual external stimuli. A hallucination may be of chemical or emotional origin and can occur in any of the five senses. Hallucinations can result from neurological as well as from psychological causes.

If your child hallucinates, consult a doctor immediately.

• *Delusions.* A delusion is a false belief which is not connected with reality and is maintained in spite of contrary advice. Several examples are *delusions of grandeur,* represented by an exaggerated sense of importance; *delusions of persecution,* which bring a false sense of being singled out for persecution; and *delusions of reference*, wrongly thinking that casual or unrelated remarks are applied to oneself.

If your child is seriously deluded, the services of a psychologist are needed quickly. However, there are a few things you can do: Avoid confronting your child with the delusions, but do listen to them; if delusions are a result of some unpleasant school experience, take the child home immediately to a calmer environment.

• *Malingering.* Malingering is the conscious stimulation of an illness used to get out of an unpleasant situation. It is a specific psychological symptom.

Malingering persons think they are, or are pretending to be, sick because they have to face something they don't want to or are afraid to face. Bribing a child is one solution for malingering, but loss of privileges is a better one. A child should not be allowed to return to play until accepting an assignment.

Determine whether your child is capable of doing the assignments objected to, and, if necessary, adjust the assignments so that the child feels competent to complete them. The assignments should not be adjusted to accommodate a faked illness, for that would only encourage future attacks of malingering.

• *Drug Addiction*. Group counseling and medical therapy are essential to the treatment of this addiction. The addict's family also needs help whether they want to help or not, because they are involved in the addict's problem whether they want to be or not. If the family doesn't accept help, they will compound the problem, and the addict's alienation will grow.

Lectures about the dangers inherent in drugs are usually nonproductive except in those instances in which former addicts describe their own experiences. The best solution is active community participation in removing drug dealers from neighborhoods, hopefully before addiction occurs.

• *Distractibility*. Children with learning disabilities are often easily distracted. Make sure that your directions are exact. You can use devices to focus your child's attention. When she reads, she may need markers to help her keep her place.

• *Perseveration*. This is a persistent and mechanical repetition of an activity. It is common with schizophrenia. Help the child overcome this problem by playing games similar to "musical chairs." With this game, children must pay close attention to the quick musical changes which pop up unexpectedly. The idea is to continually interrupt the perseverating child.

• *Impulsiveness*. This problem results from a psychic striving and is usually connected with an instinctual urge.

The reward system can be useful. You can use marks or stars to note every single act of control the child exhibits. These marks should add up to something the child wants.

• *Hyperactivity*. Some children with learning disabilities are hyperactive. Drugs are commonly used to control the disorder, yet I believe that drugs should be used by as few children as possible. No one, especially a child, should be allowed to become dependent upon chemicals. Excess activity can be an overt signal of an inner turmoil, which will remain in spite of drug taking.

The hyperactive child can often find release by physical movement. Find suitable physical activities to occupy this child during hyperactive moments. Strangely, some hyperactive children often need rest, while others seem to thrive on their own nervous energy.

Some evidence has linked the foods children eat to hyperactivity. The dyes and preservatives often added to food seem to be the culprits.

Hyperactive children often function well for a short period of time, called their "effective time." Non-effective time is the hyperactive period when adults should provide a physical activity, such as cleaning their room or running errands. I have had success with placing a rocking chair in the rear of a classroom where hyperactive children could rock off their excess energy. At other times I allowed older hyperactive children to step outside the building, where they could run around the playground.

All of the behavior modifications presented here have been used successfully. I have developed them during the thirty-two years I worked as a principal/psychologist. They have modified unacceptable behavioral problems that existed with some of the thousands of pupils I have known. They will work for you and your learning-challenged child.

CHAPTER SEVEN

Meditation Therapy

It is generally recognized that anxiety is the most common symptom exhibited by children with learning disabilities. In adults, a discussion with a good listener may result in some relief from pent-up tension. The same results might be expected in children. Children, however, tend to be extremely reticent in describing unpleasant experiences; indeed, a child's mind has difficulty in verbalizing and explaining anxiety, which is so often not even at conscious levels. Suggestions given to children when they are relaxed and sleepy have a striking effect on their mounting tension. They cause an almost instantaneous relief in the associated anxiety and a greater feeling of security so lacking in the mind of an anxious child. The results obtained by this technique are striking.

Following the use of meditative therapy, there often appears a rapid and startling change in the pathology of a child's symptoms and general outlook that can be observed by the child's teachers and parents.

As a Massachusetts school principal, I saw hundreds of children with varied learning disabilities attend guidance and remedial centers. Most of the children referred to these centers were of average or better intelligence but were failing in their work. Some of them were becoming anti-social. Most were carefully examined and returned to my school, but with only marginal help for their problems. Generally, the children still had their learning problems, which now had labels. Nonetheless, the children still had to live with these problems.

Children's problems are often complicated by environmental differences that happen even to children who live in the same house. Educational disabilities may sometimes stem from physical problems that have been resolved. Sometimes the educational disabilities remain entwined with emotional ones. Whatever the reason, children with learning disabilities live under stress that is sometimes transformed into overt symptoms: shyness, poor concentration, stuttering, and nail biting to name just a few. Some of these children give up and become apathetic. Others, with the same set of problems, become overly aggressive and disrupt their classes as a poor compensation for their academic deficits.

Children who come to school with their learning blocks already in place often have to compete with children who are confident, poised, and happy. Children with behavioral and learning disabilities often have a hard time adjusting to the rigors of normal classroom activities. They are often labeled "problem children."

As I have pointed out, children who are failing in school often think of themselves as being stupid. The way they are grouped in school emphasizes that negative self-opinion. Their school grades further emphasize the low opinion they have of themselves. Even their trek to a remedial specialist emphasizes the child's opinion, "There is something wrong with me."

Some children with learning disabilities fail in school because they have had the misfortune of being placed in the classroom of an unthinking—or worse, disturbed—teacher. These children either develop educational or emotional disabilities in their classrooms or compound the ones for which they already have predispositions. None of these children can be expected to do their best work.

A child who already has learning disabilities and perceives her home to be without love or understanding will feel safer at school, where aggressions can be acted upon. Fighting parents, overprotective parents, or dominating parents produce tensions that can disable their child. An anxious parent will often produce an anxious child. A school that rigidly adheres to grade standards and to a curriculum that is not geared to individual children—who may also be learning-challenged—will also produce an anxious child. Promotion policies that cause a student to drop behind contemporaries will handicap the failing student even more. Any student who consistently fails assignments will learn to hate not only the subject failed, but also the teacher and school. Unfortunately, hatred for the school sometimes spreads to other segments of society. Delinquency is sometimes born in school.

Incompetent teachers who use dull and ineffectual teaching methods can cause or intensify educational disabilities. Such teachers kill the academic interest of students. For instance, some teachers spend such an enormous amount of time trying to teach the phonetic elements of words that some pupils with learning disabilities lose interest in reading. These teachers usually neglect such pupils' sight vocabulary and the context clues commonly used for word recognition.

Teachers exert positive influences upon their pupils when they are sympathetic, are well trained, and properly organize the curriculum. Such teachers fit their instructions to the varied learning patterns of their pupils and not the other way around. Poor teachers should be held responsible for their failures.

An academic disability becomes ingrained if it isn't remediated. This disability creates an additional disability, the emotional circle, which I refer to as the *circle of tension*. By the time a remedial specialist is summoned to work with a troubled child, the child's problems will defy the specialist's best efforts. The circle of tension has closed the child's mind to the benefits of the specialist's help. The child is now a victim.

It is important to realize that children who have academic problems do not necessarily have emotional ones as well. In addition, there are many well-adjusted children who failed to pay attention in class or were absent at a critical teaching time. However, some children are unable to learn new and vital skills when they are introduced.

Some children with learning disabilities face personal problems that further affect their school work. Some feel that they are not wanted. These troubled children are insecure, tense, and on a slippery emotional path filled with physical disabilities: tics, bad habits, enuresis, nail biting, and asthma. The unwanted feeling may compel an anxiety reaction in one child and a delinquency reaction in another.

Children cannot be expected to sit behind their school desks when they are unhappy, worried, tense, and anxious. Nor can they sit with their minds clouded with doubts, suspicions, guilt, fear, or any other unhappy emotions associated with anxiety and be good, well-behaved students at home and at school. Moreover, a child busily attempting to work out feelings of inferiority has no chance of competing with a healthy, well-adjusted child.

Using Meditation Therapy

Meditation therapy opens up the secret or unconscious part of the brain to receive conscious thoughts. The trance-like state of meditation therapy, also called hypnotherapy, can be self-induced, induced by another person, or can occur while the subject is in a natural sleep.

Meditation therapy can help your learning-challenged child develop self-confidence. Many failures and bad habits can be eliminated. Your child can replace negative thoughts with positive ones.

It is my opinion that meditation therapy can only help; it cannot harm your child in any way. Personal control is never lost or given up to an outsider. There are only a few simple rules to follow: *This skill must be practiced. It must be made a part of the daily routine for at least two weeks.* At the beginning, it would be well to practice meditation therapy twice a day—once in the morning and again in the evening.

We rarely think about the subconscious part of our minds. We are hardly aware of the power it possesses over our lives, yet we use it constantly—to hear, to smell, to monitor the almost two thousand built-in sensors which regulate body temperature, to control sodium-potassium balance, to regulate the heartbeat, to adjust the internal gravity, to control fluids, and to manage the way we think about things. Its effectiveness depends upon its growth, its decay, and whether we have adversely affected it with drugs. We all think differently because we were conditioned to think differently. An accident—a fall from a porch or the limb of a tree—may have happened to a child, and this fall may have triggered a traumatic fear.

A traumatic fear of any kind may become an irrational phobia. Consciously the person knows that there is nothing to fear, but subconsciously he does not accept that fact because he was conditioned long before to feel afraid. We are captives of our early conditioning. If our early conditioning was negative, it could injure our health and prevent us from functioning normally. Fortunately, we can recondition ourselves to become free of our early childhood fears. Meditation therapy can begin the redemptive process immediately. It is easy to use. There is absolutely nothing to be afraid of.

Children can learn to meditate. Meditation comes from the imagination, and your learning-challenged child has a very active imagination. If you are in the habit of tucking a child in at night and saying a few pleasantries, you can add meditation therapy to your goodnight routine.

Teach your children to relax. Explain that relaxation is the opposite of tension. Show children how this works by inducing some tension into their bodies. Ask them to tighten up the muscles in their forehead, so that they induce a sense of tension. Ask them to tighten up the muscles around the eyes and across the forehead, then be sure to tell them to let all that tension go. Tense muscles produce mental anxiety. There are nerve centers located all over the body, and every muscle is connected to one or more of them. Tense muscles charge the brain with emotions of worry, fear, anxiety, and anger. These emotions can often be released by just relaxing the muscles.

Ask your child to concentrate upon the muscles around the shoulders and to raise the shoulders as high as possible. Let the child see how these tense muscles prevent relaxation. Emotionally, the child is becoming charged up. When the child understands this, be sure your instructions are to relax these muscles to let the tensions dissipate.

Do you think that your child can do anything constructive when tense? Certainly it could not be done well, if at all. If a child remains tense, sickness will eventually follow, and that sickness will be psychologically oriented. It will be a psychosomatic illness.

Your child must be relaxed both mentally and physically to enter meditation therapy. Mental imagery will help your child to relax: "Close your eyes and dream about a peaceful place. Remember the day at the beach? You fell asleep on the warm sand. Do you remember the soft warm sand and the gentle sea breeze that felt so good? You could hear the sounds of the water as it rippled along the beach. Remember the clouds drifting across the sky? You seemed to drift along with them as you fell asleep. You are relaxing now, just as you did then. You are beginning to feel wonderfully free of worries; they are leaving you now."

Continue with the induction and intone the following sequence:

1. *Breathe deeply, deeply, relax more and more, and let yourself go deeper into sleep.*

2. *Breathe more deeply than you did before; let yourself go. Let go completely.*

3. *Go deeper and deeper with each breath you take.*

4. *There is nothing to stop you now. You can go deeply into this relaxing sleep by just letting go.*

5. *Take a deep breath; let go.*

6. *Take another deep, deep, deep breath. You are beginning to relax completely. You feel drowsy. Don't hold back; let yourself go all the way.*

7. *Breathe deeply and relax. You are just about there. Just let yourself go all the way.*

8. *Take another deep breath . . . and let go. You are relaxed and drowsy.*

9. *Take a deep, deep, deep breath and allow yourself to drift off into the deepest sleep you have ever known.*

10. *Just one more deep breath, and you will drift off into deep relaxation. Nothing can stop you now; you are free to relax. Your eyes are closed, and you are ready to listen and accept these thoughts.*

The following script is available on a cassette tape. I have used it, and it has worked well with many children. However, you may want to make your own. The next few pages will tell you how.

> *"You are going to find school work easy. You will re- member the lessons, because you are going to pay attention. You are intelligent, so tests will become easier and easier. You will pay attention to the important work going on in your classroom so you will earn better grades. You are becoming so interested in what is going on in your class that you will have no time to daydream. You know that it is important to*

get a good education. You want to learn. You like people, and they are beginning to like you more and more. When your teacher assigns homework, you realize that it is in your best interest to do it well. It is wonderful to relax in this way and feel sure of your future. Your tummy aches are leaving; your headaches are leaving, too. You are beginning to feel better and better."

Meditation therapy is simple, and it can work wonders for your learning-challenged child. Later, permit your children to enter regular sleep with these messages on their minds. Let them sleep with them. The induction procedure may have put your children to sleep before you gave them your messages; that is all right. Even if your children are sound asleep, their subconscious minds are active and able to receive suggestions. When they awaken, their conscious minds serve as barriers to suggestions; they argue, rationalize, criticize, and ask questions. When the children are asleep, flashing doubts and questions are also sleeping.

You can develop special meditative messages for your child similar to the one above. I do this for each client. Here are some messages that you can alter to fit your child's specific needs.

Motivation

I believe that reinforcement rewards are signal techniques for motivation, and, when I've found that the rewards are no longer necessary to attain a specific response, I proceed to another response that I want to reinforce. Failing a child in school is a negative response to a child's effort. Obviously the child requires something more than that to continue trying. The child needs to be motivated.

Encourage children to feel better about themselves. Encourage them to feel that their family cares for them so that they will become secure and confident. Suggest that they are feeling better about school, their teachers, and fellow students. You may suggest that school is a place where they can obtain the help they need to become good students. You can remind them that each day is a new one and that they can look forward to becoming relaxed and happy in school:

"From now on you will be able to relax at school and at home, where you are loved and wanted. You are beginning to feel at ease with your family, who cares for you. Because you are comfortable at home, you will want to share in its responsibilities. You will do your best and not worry about how other people see your efforts. You can be pleased knowing that you are doing your best and that your work is continually improving.

"You are intelligent and can do many things; some of these things you can do better than others. You don't need to be concerned about remarks that your brothers and sisters have made. They have certain strengths, but so do you, and you are beginning to discover yours and you are feeling good about them. We all have certain weaknesses and strengths. I will help you to develop your strengths to their fullest extent.

"Every day and in every way you will feel better and better about yourself, and you will notice the people who do admire your strengths. You feel proud of your strengths and accomplishments. Your self-confidence will grow as you develop your talents. You are growing in strength all the time and realize that school is the place to obtain the education that you will need when you grow up. You want to get as much out of school as you can. This is for your own good, not the school's. Your ability to work with the people you meet at school will continue to develop. Your teachers are there to help you. You are in school to get as much help from

them as you can. If you happen to hear unkind comments about you or your work, you can ignore them. They can't harm you.

"Every day is a new day. You are becoming relaxed and happy at home and at school. Don't look back at yesterday, but look ahead to a better tomorrow. You have all that you need to make your tomorrow better. You are in control of yourself and your future. You will not let other people affect this. They have no power over your emotions. You control how you think about yourself, your future, your family and the opportunities that lie ahead."

Apprehension Therapy

Many children, as well as adults, are anxious about the future. Children with learning problems are especially afraid. In addition to their other fears, they fear what the future may have in store for them educationally. They wonder if they can do the work, if they can make new friends, and what the teachers will expect of them. Children who are working under a learning handicap are more apprehensive than children who are not so handicapped. Meditative therapy for apprehension problems can specifically target learning-challenged children's dependence upon other people, their short attention span, and their inability to concentrate.

"Day by day, your ability to concentrate upon your lessons will grow. You will listen to your teacher so intently that it will appear that she is talking directly to you. It will become easier for you to understand the lessons. You will listen and concentrate so intently that classroom noises will not disturb you. Nothing will disturb your concentration upon the classroom work. You will be able to see new words exactly as they are written upon the blackboard or in your textbooks.

Nothing will disturb your work. You feel good about doing the work. You feel confident. Your ability to recognize the separate parts of words will develop so well that you will be surprised at your own skills. The work will be easier, and soon you may wonder why you ever had any trouble.

"You are developing the ability to focus your attention upon specific things, and the ability to avoid paying attention to any kind of distraction. You are in control of your attention span. This control will become automatic. You will automatically know what is important and what you should be concentrating upon. Nothing will be able to disturb your power of concentration. Your power of concentration will grow stronger day by day. You will be able to concentrate longer. You will listen to what your teacher is saying. See yourself in your classroom concentrating on what your teacher is saying. . . . You are listening to your teacher. See yourself doing this. . . . See yourself watching the teacher's lips. You understand what she is talking about. See yourself at your desk. You are confident; you feel well; you are enjoying your work more and more."

The Learning Process

Information must enter your child's cognitive system and be stored for later recall. It will help your children if you attach a picture or catchy phrase to the information that is to be catalogued and stored in their brains. During World War II, I served in the Army Air Corps and had to learn the Morse Code. Our instructor gave us catchy phrases to facilitate the learning. For example, the letter *Q* consists of two dashes, one dot, and another dash. The phrase that enabled us to remember the sequence was "Pay day to day" (*daw daw ti daw*). I have already mentioned the peanut butter sandwiches of Nancy Stevenson; when you devise a script for your child's learning deficit, try to key it into a catchy phrase.

Children have wonderful imaginations. You can use their imaginations to help them overcome learning blocks. Begin by placing them in the trance state so that they can *see* themselves in their classrooms, sitting behind their desks, solving problems, raising their hands to answer questions, making mistakes and not being disturbed by them. Suggest to them, "We all make mistakes from time to time, and we learn from them." In the meditative state, they will see themselves sitting comfortably, relaxed, and enjoying pleasant feelings about their work and fellow classmates.

> *"Arithmetic is getting easy for you. It will become one of your favorite subjects because it makes sense. You are feeling good about this and enjoying pleasant experiences in your arithmetic classes. You don't hesitate to ask questions about anything that you don't understand. You wait for the right time to ask questions. Sometimes you save your questions to ask after the regular school day is over. You won't hesitate to seek help whenever you feel that you need it. You want to learn more and more."*

You may want to help your children master the number facts. You can do this by reading the numbers to them as they sleep, either naturally or in meditation. Either way will work, but the trance state is faster. You can use meditation for many other things. A friend of mine in government service uses meditation to help master the foreign languages he uses in different countries.

I have used meditation instruction, together with instruction in the awake state, to achieve dramatic success with children who exhibited the dyslexia syndrome.

Arithmetic is but one discipline that can be improved through meditation therapy. You can help your child *read* better, too. I have taught clients to go in and out of the trance state upon my signal (usually a small bell). I do this with a post-hypnotic suggestion: "When you hear me ring this special bell, you will enter the hypnotic state. When I ring it again, you will be fully awake."

Before my clients enter the trance state, I discuss the procedures I will follow. If the child has a reading problem, the session would go like this:

> *"When you were awake, you read out of this book. I want you to continue in the meditative state, but with your eyes open so that you can see the book. You are going to be able to read comfortably. Should you meet any words that you don't know, I will teach them to you, but I will only have to do this once. That will be enough, because you are going to remember them. Reading is becoming easy for you, and that's why you are beginning to like it. Soon you will be going to the library to get more books to read."*

Handwriting

If your children have trouble remembering the shapes of letters or occasionally get them backward, you can help overcome the problem the same way. When your children are deep in meditation therapy, ask them to visualize those letters that have caused problems. The children can remain in meditation, writing the letters and words correctly, but be sure to keep repeating, "This is the right way, and this is how you will make the letters from now on."

Hypnotists have been using mental imagery to help athletes for a long time. I have used the technique to help boxers and hockey players. The boxer was asked to see himself in the ring round by round and mentally fight his next bout. The same technique worked equally well for the hockey player. He played his game before the real game took place. When both athletes entered their respective arenas, they had already successfully played their games. The real thing was almost an after-the-fact event.

Spelling

Learning to spell new words can be easier for your learning-challenged children to do if you use meditation therapy. Have your children mentally "view" the words on a blackboard or on paper. As they mentally view the words, say them and spell them. Let them repeat what they have heard. If they are facing a quiz the next day, ask them to see themselves in the classroom taking the test:

> *"See how relaxed you are. You are comfortable because you know the words. As you pick up your pencil, feel the words flowing to your fingertips for you to write down. They flow easily from your mind. The right words, the right spelling, the right information comes without effort. If you need to think about the answers, all you have to do is pause for a minute, take a deep breath, let it out, and, as you relax, you will feel the answers entering your conscious mind."*

Remembering

Emotional blocks that inhibit the recall of information are problems for many students. The information they need is stored within their memory cells, but they just can't retrieve it when they have to take a test. A related problem causing recall difficulty is the length of the learning-challenged child's attention span. When the child should have been concentrating upon lessons, his mind was elsewhere and the lesson went unheeded. It was not stored because the child's mind was diverted to other factors: trouble at home, tension on the playground, a game of some kind, or television.

Good teachers give their pupils mental images to help them retain specific bits of information. For example, I will never forget the date Columbus sailed across the ocean because my teacher taught me to say, "In fourteen hundred and ninety two, Columbus sailed the ocean blue." Good teachers have a host of similar memory aids to give their pupils. Like many others, I use memory aids to help me remember the names of people I have met. I associate their names with something about them and pay particular attention to the introductions.

"It is becoming easier for you to remember things, and that's because you are paying close attention to the important things going on in your classroom. You are going to retain the knowledge you are receiving in school. This knowledge will come back to you whenever you need it. Your memory is getting better day by day, because you are concentrating on your work. You will notice this tomorrow and be delighted to watch your memory grow. The information you require will come to your mind when you need it. Unimportant things in the classroom will not distract you from concentrating upon the things you need to know. It will not distract you from your concentration and power to remember all the important things. You will be able to shut out distractions. You will not even have to think about doing this, because it is going to happen automatically.

"All your examinations will be easier, because the information you require will flow readily to your mind as you need it. Your confidence is growing day by day. If you need to think about an answer, all you have to do is pause for a minute, take a deep breath, let it out, and, as you do, the answer will appear without any effort. All the needed information will come easily to your conscious mind, because you will have done your homework. You will have prepared yourself for your examinations. Some more difficult questions may require two or more deep breaths, but that is okay. Right now, I want you to see yourself in the classroom. . . . See yourself taking a test. See how comfortable you are. . . .

See yourself taking up your pencil. . . . See your pencil moving confidently across the paper as you write the correct answers. The information flows from your brain down to your fingertips as you write. You are relaxed and comfortable."

Overcoming Frustration

Not all teachers are good for your learning-challenged child; some will be difficult, if not impossible, for you to work with. There are times when your children will be confronted with a teacher who regards them as stupid or unteachable. Unfortunately, there may not be much you can do about it. It is true that some teachers do not care about children with learning problems and have little or no patience with them. It is a fact that some teachers do have bad days and do pick on certain individuals in their classrooms.

It this happens to your vulnerable child, she may be tempted to give the teacher a bad time. If she does she will lose the battle. She must learn how to cope with the teacher's bad temperament. She must learn to continue her work regardless of her feelings for the teacher. Her purpose should be to get the best education she can, regardless of how poorly the teacher treats her. She must learn how to let a teacher's comments "roll off her back" without affecting her in any way. You, of course, must do the same thing. Your learning-challenged child must not attempt to get back at a teacher by not doing work, for that would be disastrous for the child—not the teacher. Your child must learn to do the best regardless of this further obstacle. Children need to set their own goals and standards and not let someone do this for them. They need to learn how to become confident and calm, regardless of the obstacles that face them, and with your help they can:

"When you feel threatened, frustrated, or angry, I want you to stop what you are doing and take several deep

breaths. You may need more than one breath if the situation is especially upsetting. I want you to see yourself in your classroom doing this . . . becoming calm. See yourself taking a few minutes away from the situation as you think of a peaceful and lovely scene . . . Think of our rides in the country or our trips to the beach, where you relaxed and felt good. You were free to be yourself, completely relaxed. You are slowing down and returning to the classroom, but in a relaxed condition. . . . You are feeling good; the anger has left you, and you can begin working on your assignments no matter how hard they might be. As you calm down, your confidence returns and you are able to handle the situation. You are calmly doing the work; the frustration is gone. . . . See how happy you are. You can do most of your school work without a teacher. What a wonderful feeling."

Behavior

We have already spoken of many specific kinds of misbehavior, together with prescriptions for their remediation. These prescriptions are not part of meditation therapy, even though this therapy can resolve some behavior situations. Misbehavior problems often stem from the fact that a child misunderstands others or lacks social skills. You can help your child with these difficulties in the manners already discussed.

"See yourself on the playground, where children are getting ready to play. . . . Somebody knocks you down, but you realize it could have been an accident. You are not sure. . . . The boy who knocked you down seems troubled by the accident. You assure him that you weren't hurt. You believe that it was *an accident. Now you feel good, because you didn't lose your temper; you didn't start fighting; you didn't start accusing the boy. And you may have made a friend."*

119

The above is an example of the thoughts you can suggest to your meditating child. The words you use should be tailored to fit your learning-challenged child's needs. Here is another suggested format:

> *"See yourself going to the lunch room. You would like to sit with a special friend, but you are not sure how to handle the situation. See yourself walk over to this special friend and suggest that the two of you sit together during lunch. Maybe your friend feels the same way. You talk with the other students at the table and feel good about it. . . . See yourself talking and having a good time at lunch."*

You can modify these affirmations to make them fit specific situations. The words should be adapted to your child. The appropriate suggestions for a six-year-old girl would not be appropriate for a sixteen-year-old boy. It is up to you to formulate specific affirmations for your children and their specific needs; so instead of having low self-esteem and feelings of failure, your children will see themselves as the winners they can be.

Sleep Therapy

For parents uncomfortable with the self-hypnotic aspects of meditation therapy, I would suggest the methods of sleep therapy detailed by Melvin Powers in *Mental Power*. I have used Powers's ideas for many years and have recommended them to others.

You can use sleep therapy to help your children to relax, achieve success, and feel better about themselves. Everyone is influenced by suggestion. It can be a positive or negative influence.

Suggestion can make people sick or well. A friend told me a story about an unfortunate prank played on an office worker. His associates decided to play a joke on him. Every time one of them passed his desk, he would make remarks about the worker's appearance: "Don't you feel well today?" "Do you have a headache?" "Coming down with the flu?" The worker actually got sick and had to stay home for several days.

I have mentioned that the subconscious mind is active both night and day. This is why sleep therapy works. The subconscious mind is always awake. It has to be awake to keep an individual alive. It functions automatically. We breathe, our hearts beat, the sensors detect bodily needs and sends messages to the brain so that appropriate actions may be taken without our ever having to consciously think about them.

The subconscious part of the mind can also solve problems for us as we sleep. It is another source of mental and spiritual power. When I have a difficult problem to solve, I like to sleep on it, and I frequently wake up in the morning with a fresh and better solution.

Powers offers several recording devices that can be set to come on during the night to "speak" to a sleeping individual. He calls them "sleep-o-matic units." These recording devices convert normal sleep into hypnotic sleep. When this happens, appropriate suggestions for self-improvement can be made:

> *"Continue to sleep, and as you sleep, listen to me and remember all the things I am going to tell you, because they are the things you want to hear and remember."*
>
> *[Insert the material you want the sleeper to receive and accept into his subconscious mind. When you have finished, add the following:]*
>
> *"You will continue to sleep normally, but should you need to awaken for any emergency, you will do so immediately. When you awaken, you will feel good about yourself and be thoroughly refreshed."*

Let me emphasize that the subconscious part of the mind

never sleeps. It is in constant contact with all parts of the body and is alert to receive impressions, even though the body sleeps. The conscious part of the mind serves as a barrier to suggestions, but when it sleeps, the subconscious is uninhibited and free to receive learning and healing thoughts. The subconscious mind does not discriminate, but accepts all thoughts without qualifying them. The conscious mind argues, qualifies, hesitates, doubts, is subject to emotional blocks, and "lives" according to its own standard of reference. Sleep therapy is effective because all the blocks are down, the road is open to the subconscious mind, and the mind stands ready to accept any affirmations.

Meditation therapy is another form of sleep therapy and is my own choice, because I work in a small office that is not conducive to regular sleep. But you, as a parent, may find sleep therapy to be a better choice. It *will* work. Your children's emotions are suspended when they are sleeping. There will be no roadblocks to offset the thoughts you want to instill in them.

As soon as a child has gone to sleep, one of the parents goes very quietly into the bedroom and up to the bed. A hand is slowly and gently laid on the child's forehead. Should the child stir and seem about to awake, the parent says in a low voice, "Sleep, go on sleeping, sleep soundly," repeating the phrases until the child is sound asleep once more. Then the parent, still in the same slow and quiet tones, reiterates all the improvements desirable in the child, whether from the point of view of health, sleep, work, application, conduct, or the like. When this has been done, the parent withdraws, still taking the utmost care not to awaken the child. Sleep therapy and meditation therapy are efficacious only when repeated at least eight times.

As I have already mentioned, I utilize this technique myself, sometimes with a tape recorder that goes on automatically during the night. I have found it enormously successful, and you can do the same thing for your learning-challenged child.

CHAPTER EIGHT

Case Histories

I have worked successfully with thousands of learning-challenged children. Here are some case histories of a few:

Robert

Robert was a nine-year-old boy who had failed to be promoted. He was given the Otis Lennon Mental Ability Test. This is a "paper and pencil" test, so I expected the score to be diminished by his reading disability. Even so, he gave 52 correct responses out of 80 questions. This gave him an I.Q. of 99, or about average. The boy was a bright child, and I wondered why he had failed in school.

During Robert's next visit, I administered the Iowa Every Pupil Test of Silent Reading Comprehension, Form L. Robert did not do well. In fact, he did so poorly that his test could not be scored. Out of 58 questions in the comprehensive section, Robert only answered 8 correctly. On the vocabulary part of the same test, he was only able to answer 6 out of the 40 questions. The test revealed his grade equivalent as being first grade plus eight months, but he was in the fourth grade.

After spending four years in school, Robert couldn't remember a single successful school experience other than winning a foot race on the playground. "I'm a fast runner," he stated.

When I asked Robert what he hated most in school, he replied, "I hate to fail. I don't feel good about it. Kids say things. I feel sad."

During each one of Robert's eight visits, I gave him the following affirmations to meditate upon:

"The intelligence test you took proved to us that you *are* intelligent, that you can do the work. Now, we both know this. You are not to blame for your teacher's failure to teach. You have the ability. You can do the work. You are going to complete all your work from now on. You are going to remember the words in your reading class, and you are beginning to understand them, too."

After I had given Robert eight "lessons," I did not see him again until his summer vacation, when I sent for him. He politely protested, "I don't need any more help. I am doing fine now." He was. He had lost his sad expression; he seemed to be a new boy. He repeated the test he had done so poorly on a few months earlier. Here are both results:

	Before	*After*
Reading Comprehension	too low to be scored	grade 3.3
Vocabulary	too low to be scored	grade 4.2
Total Response	grade 1.8	grade 3.7

Robert had received no therapy other than that which he received in those eight meditative sessions. The results were fantastic.

◆　◆　◆

John

John was a high school student, the oldest of four children. He didn't get along well with any member of his family, and he also had trouble getting along with his teachers. He felt that he was always being picked on. John had many physical fights with his siblings. In school, he identified with those peers who were not interested in getting good marks. John wanted to be liked, but he admitted, "I don't know the right thing to do."

After a stomach ache was relieved by meditative therapy, John readily accepted the idea of therapy. I used Emile Coure's famous thoughts, "Day by day I am getting better in every way." John's school-related tensions left him. His confidence, ability, and academic standing increased dramatically.

After a couple of lessons, he joyfully exclaimed, "I got 90% on my chemistry exam. The teacher was surprised and thought I had cheated. I did not!" Only a couple of weeks earlier, John's parents had received a deficiency report that he was failing chemistry.

John loved sports, especially hockey. His great interest in hockey led to his return to the meditative sessions. Just before one of his games, he asked for help. While he was in meditation, I intoned, "See yourself playing the game. . . . Can you see yourself out there on the ice?"

John nodded.

"Feel the effect of driving the puck home."

John's body moved slightly, as he followed the thought.

"See yourself driving the puck home again and again. See yourself skating confidently, feeling good about your game."

During John's next visit, I asked, "By the way, how did your hockey game go?"

"Wonderful! I got two of the five goals we scored that night."

John was especially proud, for he was the only sophomore playing hockey on a team comprised of seniors.

I asked about another chemistry test he had recently taken.

"I was relaxed. The test was a breeze, and would you believe that I got a hundred? The first one I have ever had."

John graduated from high school and went on to college, where he majored in business. He is now the president of his company.

Randy

Randy appeared to be perfectly confident and well adjusted, but he wasn't. Randy had enuresis (involuntary urination) and was a failing student. When I asked him to tell me about the things he had done well in school, he couldn't think of anything, but he had much to say about his failures. He had not been promoted.

"I think about it a lot," he said. "My friends were promoted, but I wasn't because I am stupid."

Randy took the blame for his failure. He did not blame his teachers, his family, or the school. "I am stupid," he insisted.

Randy needed a little help reading the test questions, but my help didn't affect the scores. Randy had a few adjustment problems. His mother had already revealed that the boy didn't get along well with other children. He was quick to lose his temper, and he hit others when things didn't go his way. Randy only wanted to play with other children when they agreed to play his way. Was this his way of regaining some of the status he had lost in school?

School was not a magic learning place for Randy. It had failed him, but he thought *he* had failed *it*. As a result, he didn't want to go to school anymore. He wanted to stay home, where he felt safe from ridicule.

He was a bed-wetter and had been for as long as he could

remember. No one told me about it, but his mother told him that I was going to help him overcome this problem. She had done everything she could to cure the child. He had seen medical doctors, and his bed had been equipped with an electric blanket that woke up everyone in the house *except* Randy, who didn't seem to mind the noise or the wet blanket. The trouble with electrical blankets of the type Randy used was that they sounded their alarms *after* the fact.

To me, Randy was a charming child. Perhaps I found him charming because I didn't have to live with him—he was the neighborhood terror. He played aggressively, was accused of putting sand in the gas tank of a neighbor's car, and became unduly interested in some neighborhood fires. His mother gave up her job to look after him. It is interesting to note that his fire interests ceased after she stayed home to spend more time with him. Could his bed-wetting activity have been connected to his interest in fires? Was he subconsciously putting them out?

Randy had a pleasant personality and found it easy to make friends, but these friendships did not last long because of his colorful vocabulary. When his new friends showed off their newly acquired vocabulary around their own homes, their parents put an end to these developing friendships. As a result, Randy had to play with much older boys who may have helped him develop his vocabulary in the first place.

Randy took the Frostig Development Test of Visual Perception. He did poorly. He was in the lowest quartile. He hadn't learned much of anything in the first grade, not much in the second grade, and was doing little in the third grade.

I was pleased to discover that, even with his tremendous educational handicap, Randy was a bright boy. His I.Q. was 98, in spite of his great perceptual handicap and a reading ability that was hardly of first-grade level.

During one of his visits he informed me that he had stopped bed-wetting. This revelation surprised me since I had not been aware of the problem. It turned out that he believed he was receiving therapy for enuresis. He was cured because he expected it, but I had never said a word to him about it.

Randy was seriously dyslexic. "And I have trouble with numbers, especially the fives. I make them backward."

Randy came to my office eight times. His therapy included these affirmations: "You are an intelligent boy. We proved that with the intelligence test. I want you to remember that for as long as you live."

Randy read for me while he was in the trance state and made some mistakes. I corrected his mistakes. Occasionally, I awakened him so that he could repeat the exercise when fully awake. These sessions included the following: "Tomorrow in school you will read just as well as you have done here tonight."

Randy had trouble with numbers. He did some arithmetic for me, and he seemed to be unable to make some of his numbers correctly. His mother had informed me, "He has always made some of his numbers backwards. I guess he sees them that way."

When Randy was deep in meditation, I asked him to open his eyes and write some numbers for me. He made some of them backwards. While still in meditation, he was corrected. We repeated the exercise a couple of times until he was able to make his numbers the right way. We did the exercise while he was in and out of meditation. When he was in the meditative state he was told, "You see, you *can* make your numbers the right way. You are going to remember this and make them the right way from now on." The meditation therapy was joined with Fernald's technique. The child's hand was guided through the exercise a few times. Within minutes he no longer needed this help.

The following week, Randy was especially eager to see me, for he had much to tell.

"My mother noticed that I was writing numbers correctly and asked about it. I told her that I was making them correctly because I was seeing you."

He proudly did some arithmetic problems for me without a single mistake. He had overcome his dyslexic problem *in one short lesson*.

I have lost count of the number of children I have helped using meditation therapy. All of their lives were changed for the better. Some of the children achieved a complete success. This was not true for all of them; however, the range of success was slanted in favor of complete success.

Affirmations for self-improvement can come from the individual in the meditative state or from another person. The change occurs when the individual accepts the affirmations. In every case, the curative power is within the individuals themselves.

The children I saw lived under varying levels of stress. These children learned to live with stress, to rise above the unpleasant conditions, or to cope with a stressful situation that could not be changed. When these children entered the meditative state, they relaxed and allowed my positive affirmations to take root and grow. Positive things happened to them as they released their negative self-esteems.

Every experience we encounter forms a frame of reference for succeeding experiences. These "programming experiences" can be both negative and positive. We are fortunate because negative reference frames can be eliminated and replaced with positive ones. Everything that has been learned can be unlearned, and this is important to meditative therapy.

The previous negative conditioning will try to reassert itself. When it does, it can be quickly erased.

Every student with whom I have worked achieved some measure of success by using meditation therapy. There have been no unpleasant surprises. This therapy has been successful in modifying behavior and personality aberrations. Each child has become more independent and gained a better self-impression.

Most of the time, I utilized tape recordings as a meditative aid. Some of my recordings contain a standard message, but if time permitted I made a special tape for each individual, patterned for specific needs.

A group of neighborhood boys, ranging in age from eight to twelve years, came to my home once a week for twelve weeks. The boys stretched out on the floor, closed their eyes, and listened to me. Their parents reported that their children did perform better in school and at home after these sessions. There were no unpleasant experiences.

The children kept notebooks about their experiences:

"The teacher gave us a test booklet and expected us to do 50 to 60 pages. I did 106 and could have gone on."

"I liked it, because I was so relaxed and comfortable."

"It felt like I was floating upon some kind of ocean."

"Totally relaxed."

"I was mostly affected in school. I have been improving and answering the teacher's questions."

"My life is better."

"I am relaxed and have been doing good."

The following is the transcript of the tape I used for these children:

"Close your eyes and dream about the most relaxed and peaceful place you can remember—a special place where you rested and felt good about yourself, perhaps a beach with only a few people about and the sun going down. You fell asleep to dream pleasant thoughts. The sand was warm. The gentle breeze warmed your body. You can hear the peaceful sound of waves rippling and rolling sand along the beach. You were relaxed and at peace with the world. You watched the soft clouds drift by and you seemed to drift along with them. You let go then, and you can do that now. Don't hold back, just let yourself go and enter a sweet peace. You are free of tensions, absolutely relaxed, dreaming

about the soft clouds drifting by, and letting your mind drift along with them. Your worries are leaving you. You are resting in your private place. You can almost hear the sounds of water rippling along your beach. I am going to count to ten, and I would like you to take a deep breath every time I count. This will help you go deeper into relaxation. You are free of anxieties. Nothing will disturb you. You are free of fear.

"One. Take a deep breath and relax completely.

"Two. Take another deep breath and go deeper into relaxation.

"Three. Breathe deeply and enjoy deep relaxation.

"Four. Take another deep breath and let go.

"Five. Take a deep breath. Feel yourself drift deep into relaxation.

"Six. Take a deep breath and drift deep into the most relaxed state you can. Go all the way.

"Seven. Deep breath. Deep relaxation. Let go completely. Nothing can bother you, so relax and let go. You are free of tensions and anxieties and are enjoying peace.

"Eight. Take another deep breath and let go. You are feeling relaxed and drowsy. You feel sleepy, and it's all right for you to feel that way.

"Nine. Take another deep breath and relax. Drift off into this wonderful, relaxing state of mind where you have no anxieties, only peace of mind.

"Ten. Just one more deep breath. Nothing can stop you from drifting off into deep relaxation. Your eyes are closed, and you feel sleepy. You are ready to allow sleep to come. There is nothing to it. All you have to do is let go.

"School is becoming easier, because your ability to concentrate is increasing. You know that you are intelligent and can remember the things you learn in school. You will pay attention and do less daydreaming. You know that you

need a good education, so you want to obtain all the education you can. You like people, and you know that most people like you, and that you can get along with just about everybody. You don't mind doing your homework, because you realize that it is in your own best interest.

"All your tensions are fading away. You are feeling better about yourself. You can open your eyes and awaken feeling fine."

Tests Used in American Schools

Many tests are used in the American school system to determine specific learning disabilities. The type of test used in a particular system often depends on the favorite of the resident psychologist. I, for example, prefer the Binet Intelligence Test over the Wechsler Scale of Intelligence, but other psychologists prefer the Wechsler.

Among the hundreds of tests are a few primary ones:

Assessment of Children's Language Comprehension (ACLC)

The ACLC is used for young children who have trouble assimilating language. The child points to a picture corresponding to the words spoken by the examiner. The child does not have to say anything; he has only to point to the corresponding picture.

Bender Gestalt Test

The Bender Gestalt can be given to both adults and young children. It determines how well the subject takes in visual information, absorbs it, and puts it on paper. The subjects are given nine different designs to examine and copy. They can take all the time they need. I used this test to screen students suspected of having brain damage. The students who failed the test were sent to a neurologist.

Benton Visual Retention Test

The Benton test can be given to anyone who is eight years of age or older. It tests visual perception and memory. The subject is shown ten cards marked with designs and then is asked to reproduce the designs from memory.

Botel Reading Inventory

This is easy to give to elementary-age children. The children are asked to identify certain words, provide antonyms for them, and to decipher some new words.

Carrow Elicited Language Inventory

The Carrow test can be given to any child between the ages of three and seven and is intended to determine how well these students use grammar. A sentence is read to the subject, who is asked to repeat the sentence, but with corrected grammar using substitutions, additions, transpositions, reversals, and omissions.

Clinical Evaluation of Language Functioning (CELF)

This interesting test is used throughout the grades. Its purpose is to locate problems in these various language areas:

• *Word and sentence structure*. The pupil is asked to select a picture representing the sentence read by the examiner.

• *Processing words*. The examiner reads a series of words to the child, who is asked to identify those words that don't belong in the group.

• *Linguistic concepts.* The pupil is asked to select a picture representing what the examiner has said.

• *Relations and ambiguities.* The student answers yes or no to a series of questions of relationships. For example, "Are grandparents older than their children? Is a wing to a bird as a wheel is to a cart?"

• *Oral directions.* The pupil is given a series of directions that range from simple to complex.

• *Spoken paragraphs.* The examiner reads a series of short paragraphs to the pupil, who then answers questions about the reading.

• *Word series.* The pupil is asked to relate common items in sequence; for example, the numbers from one to ten.

• *Confrontation of names.* The pupil looks at colors and shapes and is asked to identify them.

• *Word associations.* The pupil is asked to think of all the words that belong in a given category.

• *Model sentences.* The examiner reads a sentence, and the subject is asked to recite it just as it was said. The examiner notes all omissions and substitutions.

• *Formulated sentences.* The student is given one word and is asked to use it in a sentence.

• *Sounds of speech.* Two similar words are read to the subject, who is asked to tell if they are the same; for example, *set* and *sat.*

• *Making the sounds of speech.* The student is asked to complete a sentence missing a word that begins with a specific sound; for example, "I like to ride in my father's _____." This sentence compels the pupil to make the *K* sound in the response *car.*

Detroit Learning Aptitude Test

The Detroit test can be used with subjects from age three to adult. It diagnoses areas of learning disability that need remediation. There are eight tasks involved:

1. *Reasoning and comprehension.* The subject is shown eight absurd pictures and is asked, "What is silly about these pictures?"

2. *Practical judgment.* The subject is asked to put an X into circles as quickly as possible. The subject is told to do certain tasks and to follow directions.

3. *Verbal ability.* The subject is asked to say as many words as possible in a limited amount of time.

4. *Time and space relationships.* The subject is shown a design. It is quickly removed from her sight and she is asked to reproduce it. There are some disarranged pictures that have been cut up. The subject is to tell in what order they would be in proper arrangement.

5. *Number ability.* The subject is asked to count with and without objects, identify larger and smaller objects, and so on.

6. *Auditory attentive ability.* Words and syllables are said to the subject, who has to repeat them in the order given or in the right order.

7. *Visual attentive ability.* The subject is shown cards with pictures. The cards are removed from the subject's sight. She then has to recall them.

8. *Motor ability.* The subject's motor speed and precision is noted as she performs the above tasks.

Duke Test of Intellectual Ability

There are two editions of this test. One is for elementary school children and one is for high school students and adults. When used carefully, the Duke test can determine the subject's I.Q. An I.Q. of 110 or better is usually needed for success in college. (Results correlate well with the Binet.)

Duke Personality Survey

Twenty-one personality traits are surveyed. These traits are defined as follows:

1. *Leadership*. The subject is sure of himself. He makes his own decisions.

2. *Indecisive*. The subject lets someone else take the lead. He lacks confidence. He is a listener.

3. *Accountable*. The subject remains steadfast to a task, no matter what the obstacles. He is responsible.

4. *Unreliable*. The subject cannot be counted upon to finish a job. He is not dependable.

5. *Confident*. The subject is trustworthy. People can rely on him, and he is self-reliant.

6. *Tense*. The subject is anxious, nervous, and easily upset.

7. *Friendly*. The subject is accessible, amicable, and enjoys having people around him.

8. *Retiring*. The subject can work well with others, but normally avoids social contact.

9. *Prudent*. The subject does not take unnecessary chances. He thinks before acting or speaking.

10. *Careless*. The subject loves excitement. He takes risks and makes quick decisions.

11. *Creative*. The subject likes to think things out. He likes to create something new out of existing materials.

12. *Tolerant*. The subject has a long-suffering disposition, indulgent and liberal.

13. *Critical*. The subject is easily annoyed. He lacks faith in others and is inclined to be picky.

14. *Active*. The subject is full of energy and has a great capacity for work.

15. *Lethargic*. The subject tires easily, works at a slow pace, and is somewhat dull.

16. *Fearful*. The subject is apprehensive and inclined to look with awe at new people and things.

17. *Decisive*. The subject is prompt, conclusive, and tends to put an end to uncertainty.

18. *Outgoing*. The subject is inclined to go out of his way and to excel in most things. He meets people well.

19. *Follower*. The subject is inclined to move or act under the leadership of someone else.

20. *Impetuous*. The subject has much energy and is inclined to act upon impulse and incentive.

21. *Temperamental*. The subject is sensitive, easily excited, and changeable.

Duke Occupational Survey

This test can suggest several occupations well suited to the student. The evolvement chart will enable the subject to plot these occupations into three groups. The first group usually requires college training. The second group usually requires technical school training. The third group only requires high school training.

The Educational Evaluation

This test is used with five- and six-year-old children to identify problems that might exist with their basic knowledge, perception, and directionality. It asks the child's name and address, moving from that to language development, discrimination, and perception of words. It inquires about words for parts of the body and notes the ability to count and identify numbers. It reveals a child's memory, tactile perception, and directional concepts.

Flannagan Aptitude Classification Test

This test predicts a student's success in vocations by examining her inherent mental and physical abilities. There are group and individual aptitude tests, consisting of batteries that permit a counselor to suggest several vocational choices that fit the individual's aptitudes.

Goodenough Harris Drawing Test

This is a mental ability test for children whose ages run from three to fifteen years. A child is asked to draw a person. The test is based upon the idea that a more mature person will include more details in the drawing and is scored by the number of body parts the child includes in the drawing.

Illinois Test of Psycholinguistic Abilities (ITPA)

The ITPA is used with children ages two through ten years. It identifies problems in linguistics (language areas).

Jordon Left-Right Reversal Test

The Jordan test is used with children ages five through twelve years to determine whether the brain reverses information. The child has to pick out letters and numbers that are printed in reverse.

Key Math Diagnostic Test

This test is given to children from preschool through grade six. It determines mathematical skills and weaknesses and indicates what the remediation should be.

Lindemood Auditory Conceptualization Test

This test is given to children from kindergarten through grade twelve. It evaluates the subject's ability to sort out speech sounds and to perceive numbers. The teacher says a sound pattern, and the subject arranges colored blocks to represent the sound pattern.

Marianne Frostig Developmental Test of Visual Perception

I have used this test many times and found it useful with

children from kindergarten through grade six. It evaluates eye-motor coordination, recognizing shapes, positions of shapes, and spatial relations (changing letter order in different words).

McCarthy Scales of Children's Abilities

This is used as a pre-kindergarten screening test and in the elementary grades to evaluate intellectual and motor development. It examines the separate components of intelligence and adds them together to give a "General Cognitive Score." It offers separate scores for the verbal, perceptual, and quantitative aspects of intelligence, plus a total score.

Meeting Street School Test

This is used in kindergarten and first grade to identify children who have potential learning disabilities. The test examines several areas:

• *Behavioral.* This scale includes: cooperation, attention, self-monitoring, motor control, use of a pencil, eye control, speech, and the use of grammar.

• *Motor Patterning.* The pupil is asked to hop, skip, clasp hands, dance, follow directions, and turn left and right.

• *Visual Perception.* The pupil is asked to match items, shapes, and numbers. He is asked to copy shapes and follow directions which include things that are behind, above, around, and under.

• *Language.* The pupil is asked to repeat words and sounds, to count objects and numbers backward and forward, to make up a story, and to complete sequences.

Minnesota Spatial Test

This test is used with high school students and adults to assess their ability to match objects. The subject is shown a form board from which he is to remove blocks and place them in another form board as quickly as possible.

Neurological Dysfunctions of Children

The test was designed to help a psychologist determine whether he should refer a child to a neurologist for a full examination. The instrument is for children between the ages of three and ten years. The subject is asked to do a number of tasks: walk a straight line, hop, walk on tiptoe, touch the nose with a finger tip, and make sequential movements with the hands. The circumference of the child's head is measured to see if the size is normal, and the child's personal history is examined for injuries or accidents that might have affected the motor functions.

Otis-Lennon Mental Ability Test

There are several editions of this test for varying ages so it can be used to evaluate students from kindergarten through high school. This test assesses reading achievement, reading comprehension, spelling, arithmetic and general information.

Peabody Picture Vocabulary Test

I enjoy giving this test because it is as fun for me as it is for the student. One version can be used with children as young as two. It can also be used with adults. It measures general intelligence, but it is primarily a language test. The student doesn't have to be able to read to take this test; she only has to point at pictures illustrating the meaning of the words the examiner reads to her.

Quick Neurological Screening Test

This test can be used with subjects from kindergarten age through adulthood. It identifies those who are neurologically impaired. The test examines the auditory, visual, and motor-sensory skills.

Raven Progressive Matrices

This test is designed to examine the mental ability of people age eight through sixty-five. The interesting thing about this test is the absence of talking or writing. The subject looks at a series of abstract pictures and solves problems with them. The problem solving progresses in difficulty.

Slingerland Screening Tests

This is used extensively in grades one through six to identify children with difficulties in reading, writing, spelling, and speaking. The Slingerland examines seven tasks:

1. *Visual motor coordination.* The student is asked to copy a paragraph or a few words from a chart on the wall. The work is examined for letter formation, reversals, inversions, transpositions, omissions, substitutions, spacing, use of space, and handwriting.

2. *Visual perception-memory.* The student is shown words, letters, and numbers, and, on another page, is asked to identify the previously shown words.

3. *Visual discrimination.* The student looks at a word at the top of the list and seeks another one just like it somewhere down the list.

4. *Visual memory linked with motor coordination.* The student is shown letters, words, numbers, and shapes. When these are removed from view, he is asked to reproduce them from memory.

5. *Auditory memory linked with motor ability.* Words, numbers, and letters are read to the student, who then must write what he has heard.

6. *Auditory visual discrimination.* Words, letters, and

numbers are read to the student, who has to select what has been read from a line of four items.

7. *Auditory memory to motor ability*. The psychologist reads a word to the student, who selects either the beginning or the ending sound of that word.

Slosson Intelligence Test

This is a quick way to determine intelligence for individuals ranging from early childhood through adulthood. The test consists of a series of physical activities, analogies, questions, definitions, comparisons, vocabulary, general information, and drawing geometric figures.

Stanford Binet Intelligence Test

This test can be used with two-year-old children, as well as adults. The test was originated in France by Dr. Binet to determine which children could best benefit from a formal education. There are five separate tasks evaluated:

1. *General comprehension*.

2. *Visual motor ability*. Children work with building blocks and pictures. Older subjects are asked to cut and fold paper into designs.

3. *Arithmetic reasoning*. Most of the calculations are done in the student's head.

4. *Vocabulary and verbal fluency*. At the lowest levels the subjects are asked to identify common objects. The test advances in complexity when the subject is asked to explain the meaning of proverbs and codes.

5. *Judgment and reasoning*. The subject compares objects, answers questions, identifies foolish statements, and solves problems.

Verbal Language Development Skills

This test determines the "language age" of subjects from ages one through sixteen. The examiner doesn't have to work directly with the child, but interviews someone familiar with the child's speech habits.

This array of psychological tests is not exhaustive. There are hundreds of psychological tests on the market. I have mentioned just a few that have been used at one time or another in my own schools.

Resources

**The Association for Children
  With Learning Disabilities**
4156 Library Road
Pittsburgh, Pennsylvania 15234

**The Council for Exceptional
  Children**
1420 Association Drive
Reston, Virginia 22091

**The Child Study Association
  of America**
50 Madison Avenue
New York, New York 10010

**The Foundation for Children
  with Learning Disabilities**
99 Park Avenue
New York, New York 10016

The Children's Defense Fund
122 "C" Street, NW
Washington, D.C. 20001

**The Home and School
  Institute**
201 16th Street, NW
Washington, D.C. 20001

**The Council for Basic
  Education**
725 15th Street, NW
Washington, D.C. 20005

**The National Association for
  Gifted Children**
2070 County Road, H Street
St. Paul, Minnesota 55112

**The National Committee for
  Citizens in Education**
410 Wilde Lake, Village Green
Columbia, Maryland 21044

**The National School
  Volunteer Program**
300 N. Washington Street
Alexandria, Virginia 22314

**The National Parent Teachers
  Association**
700 N. Rush Street
Chicago, Illinois 60611

Glossary

Acalculia: The inability to do arithmetic and to comprehend concepts represented by numbers.

Anomia: The inability to name objects even though they may be clearly seen.

Aphasia: Refers to a loss or impairment of speech, writing, or signs. Impairment or loss of the ability to comprehend spoken or written language. It is from the Greek word *phasia*, which means "to speak." When the prefix *a-* is added, the meaning is changed to "without (or in this case, less) speech."

Attentional Deficit Disorder: A new term applied to what was called "Minimal Brain Dysfunction," referring to a syndrome that affects children, primarily boys. The causes are not known and there is no single symptom to effect a diagnosis. A stricken child usually has average or better intelligence and demonstrates learning and/or behavioral abnormalities. He may be hyperactive or clumsy and have particular trouble with reading and writing.

Auditory-visual integration: The ability to remember printed letters that mean specific sounds in words or the reverse.

Binet Test: An intelligence test that can be used for children and adults. Also called the Simon-Binet Test and the Stanford-Binet Test.

Central Nervous System (CNS): The brain and the spinal cord.

Cerebral Dominance: The supremacy of one cerebral hemisphere over the other. Right-handedness is thought to indicate that the left cerebral hemisphere is dominant.

Cognition: Knowledge, including awareness and judgment. Perception, memory, introspection, thinking, awareness of objects, and thought are all included.

Congenital: Refers to a condition at birth which may be the result of faulty development, infection, or injury in the uterus.

Decoding: The process of translating unfamiliar material into a familiar form, as in the ability to read or turn unfamiliar written symbols into known spoken words.

Developmental Aphasia: Describes a characteristic of individuals who are not able to put their thoughts together to say the things they want to say and may not be able to understand what is being said. This disorder can develop from a head injury or a disease.

Directionality: In educational psychology, this refers to the normal left, normal right, or up and down. Young people sometimes have a problem reading letters or words as they should be read, left to right. For some reason, a few individuals have a tendency to work from the bottom to the top.

Dominance: Educational psychologists use this term to identify the preferential use of one eye over the other or one hand over the other. The right-handed individual usually has a dominant right eye. The reverse is equally true, but this does not necessarily mean that one eye or hand is stronger or better than the other. It may simply indicate which side of the brain approaches a problem first. We also refer to one hemisphere of the brain as being dominant, but again, this does not suggest that one side is better than the other.

Dyscalculia: A difficulty learning to do arithmetic. The difficulty consists in comprehending the relationships between mathematical concepts and symbols.

Dysfunction: The prefix *dys-* refers to the absence, or trouble with, an ability. The term implies that something is functioning poorly.

Dysgraphia: Comes from the Greek word *graphein*, which means "to write." The individual with this problem has an inability to write properly. Dysgraphia may be part of a language disorder caused by a disturbance of the parietal lobe or of the motor system.

Dyslexia: From the Greek *lexical*, which refers to words, vocabulary, and the use of words. The prefix *dys-* indicates that trouble exists with words. It does not necessarily mean that an individual sees a reversal of the letters in words or that some of the letters are seen upside down, but this may happen. The medical profession suggests it is an inability to read with an understanding due to a brain lesion. Dyslexia seems to be more prevalent in boys.

Dysphasia: An inability to coordinate speech and arrange words in their proper order.

Encoding: In reading, this refers to a child's ability to write, take dictation, and turn the spoken word into an acceptable written code.

Exceptional child: Any child who deviates from normal mental, physical, or social characteristics to such an extent that modified educational practices are necessary for him to develop to his maximum capacity.

Hyperactive: The prefix *hyper-* means "more than normal," so this word indicates that something, or someone, is overactive. In education, this adjective describes the abnormally increased activity of some children, which often includes constant motion, distractibility, and a low tolerance for frustration.

Hyperkinetic: This is used interchangeably with *hyperactive* and means abnormally increased muscular action.

Kinesthesia: The sense by which position, weight, and movement are identified.

Kinesthetic Method: A method of teaching that has a child trace the word to be learned with her finger and say it as she traces it. This method was used by both Fernald and Montessori.

Kleptomania: Compulsive stealing without any regard as to need or the intrinsic value of the stolen objects, which often have an unconscious, symbolic value only to the subject.

Glossary

Laterality: As used in education, this refers to individuals' dominant use of the right or left side of any parts of their bodies.

Linguistics: The study of language, its units, nature, modifications, origin, and structure.

Maturation: The growth and development that results in maximum intellectual and emotional development along with emerging personal and behavioral characteristics.

Minimal Brain Dysfunction: Another term for "Attentional Deficit Disorder."

Mirror writing: The tendency to write from right to left as the words might be seen in a mirror.

Multi-disciplinary team: Some schools have a group of people who examine troubled children and make specific decisions to help them. Several disciplines, or branches of learning, are apt to be involved in this task, including school psychology, classroom teaching, special needs, administration, and medical.

Multisensory: Using more than one of the five senses at the same time. In teaching, it refers to methods that appeal to sight, hearing, and touch in combination.

Neuropsychology: The study that deals with the relationship between behavior and the nervous system in normal organisms. This is usually done with lower animals.

Operant Conditioning: A type of learning in which the learner performs a specific act because that act will produce a reward. Also called "instrumental conditioning."

Perception Span: The number of discrete elements that can be remembered after hearing or seeing them only once. This sometimes forms an element in intelligence testing.

Perception: An awareness of objects, relationships, or qualities.

Phobia: An obsessive, unrealistic fear of an external object or situation. This fear is believed to arise from a displacement of an internal conflict to an external object that is somehow related to the conflict.

Phonetics: The system of speech sounds of a language.

Play therapy: A psychotherapeutic approach to children's emotional disorders.

Psychosomatic: The word denotes the interaction of the mind (*psyche*) and the body (*soma*). It is commonly used to refer to illnesses pertaining to the mind-body relationships in which the manifestations are primarily physical but have an emotional etiology.

Reversals: Errors often made by beginning readers, in which single letters may be turned around or the order of letters within words is reversed (*was* for *saw*).

Rotation: Turning letters upside down or at incorrect angles (for example, *b* for *p*).

Syndrome: A group of symptoms or indications that, considered together, characterize a disease or other abnormal condition.

Syntax: The way in which words are put together to form phrases, clauses, or sentences.

Tactile: Pertaining to the sense of touch.

Trauma: A psychological or physical injury.

Word blindness: A nineteenth- and early-twentieth-century term for dyslexia.

Word-attack skills: A term used to describe a reader's ability to analyze an unknown word by breaking it down into syllables or other phonic elements to arrive at its pronunciation and meaning.

Bibliography

Ambrose, Gordon. *Hypnotherapy with Children*. London: Staples Press.

Bannatyne, Alexander. *Reading: An Auditory Vocal Process*. San Rafael: Academic Therapy Publications.

Blanco, Ralph E., and David F. Bogacki. *Prescriptions for Children with Learning and Adjustment Problems*. Springfield: Charles C. Thomas, 1988.

Buros, Oscar K., ed. *Mental Measurements Yearbooks*. Lincoln: University of Nebraska.

Delcato, Carl H. *A New State for the Child with Reading Problems*. New York: David McKay.

Doman, Glenn. *How to Teach Your Baby to Read*. New York: Random House, 1990.

Dorland's Medical Dictionary. New York: W. B. Saunders Co.

Duke, Robert E. *Hypnotherapy for Troubled Children*. Far Hills,

NJ: New Horizon Press, 1984.

Eden, John. *The Eye Book*. New York: The Viking Press.

Flesch, Rudolph. *Why Johnny Can't Read*. New York: Harper & Row, 1986.

Frostig, Marianne. *Reading Performance and How to Achieve It*. Syracuse: Syracuse University Press.

Funk, Wilfred. *Six Weeks to Words of Power*. New York: Pocket Books.

Gardner, William I. *Learning and Behavior Characteristics of Exceptional Children and Youth*. Boston: Houghton Mifflin, 1977.

Gattegno, Caleb. *Teaching Reading with Words in Color*. New York: Educational Solutions.

Kephart, F. L. *The Slow Learner in the Classroom*. New York: Charles E. Merrill.

Lynn, Roa, et al. *Learning Disabilities: An Overflow of Theories, Approaches, and Politics*. New York: The Free Press, 1979.

Maslow, Abraham. *Motivation*. New York: Harper & Row.

Myers, Patricia L., and Donald Hammill. *Methods for Learning Disorders*. New York: John Wiley.

Owens, Freyda. *Learning Disabilities, A Psychological Perspective*. Cambridge, MA.

Bibliography

Powers, Melvin. *Mental Power Through Sleep Suggestion*. Hollywood: Wilshire

Ross, Alan O. *Psychological Aspects of Learning Disorders of Children*. New York: McGraw, 1976.

Seeman, Bernard. *Your Sight*. Boston: Little, Brown.

Simpson, Eileen. *Reversals: A Personal Victory Account of Victory over Dyslexia*. Boston: Houghton Mifflin.

Spalding, Romalda B., and Walter T. Spalding. *Writing Road to Reading: A Modern Method of Phonics for Teaching Children to Read*. New York: Morrow, 1972.

Stevenson, Nancy. *The Natural Way to Reading*. Boston: Little, Brown.

Synthesis of ASCD Resolutions Through 1984. Alexandria: Association for Supervision & Curriculum Development.

U.S. Department of Education, Office of Research and Development, Washington, DC.

Wallace, Gerald, and James A. McLoughlin. *Learning Disabilities, Concepts and Characteristics*. New York: John Wiley, 1979.

Wright, Robert, and Robert Alley. *A Profile of the Ideal Teacher*. Reston: NASSP 1904 Association Bulletin.

Index